PHIL O'BRIEN spent his early years on a remote cattle station in the Northern Territory. But a severe drought brought him and his family down to Adelaide - Security and the suburbs never really appealed to him and when he was old enough to drive he blew out of town and headed bush. Twenty five years and about two hundred jobs later, Phil's still out there roaming around going from job to job and place to place and meeting all sorts of characters along the way. Described by Westpac Bank as 'nomadic' he is a financial disaster with no fixed address - but shit! - whichever way you look at it he's got some great stories to tell! And in his own way Phil has turned drifting around Outback Australia into an art form.

The 'Minor Successes' of a Bloke That Never Had a Real Lot of Luck

PHIL O'BRIEN

This book is dedicated
To my late mate Stewy Dhummurangi
A rough diamond
Let your spirit go unhindered

Cover, art work and typesetting - Geoff Morrison,
Bodgie Graphics, 16 Cove Street, Birchgrove, NSW 2041.

Printed by - Griffen Press Australia

ISBN 978-0-9580667-2-3

ACKNOWLEDGMENTS

A special thanks to my family for always helping out with food and accommodation every time I blow into town. Without their help I don't think I would have
been able to compile this book in such comfort. Also my sister Marilyn who has
gone above and beyond the call of duty in helping me to proof read the wild
and rocky manuscript. Once again thanks to my mate Geoff Morrison of
Bodgie Graphics, and sorry about that croc attack last time you came up to the
Northern Territory. Last but not least, thanks to all the lovers of fine literature
out there that have bought my books, and to those who are about to read ...
I salute you.

'Whilst trying to attain the unattainable
Don't forget …
Achieve the Achievable'

Author Phil O'Brien. age 3. at Tempe Downs Station 'looking for some action!'

Contents

TWO SILVER BREAM IN THE MOONLIGHT

IT WAS BUILD UP TIME in the tropical Top End of the Northern Territory. Hot, sticky, really bloody hot and steadily growing hotter. Humidity was on the way up and the air was that heavy it was getting hard to suck it up and get it down into your lungs.

The long windy dry had left the country parched and burnt out, but the wet season rains were still several weeks away. This is what the locals call the suicide season, the gap between the dry and the wet; it's a tough time for both man and nature.

If you listened carefully you could hear the bush panting, gasping, desperate for the cooling monsoon, desperate to move into the next cycle of life, but rain is the trigger and until it lets go every living thing has just got to hold on.

My part in all this was simple, a week ago I'd been a little bit charged up at a party in old Darwin town, yarning about the fact I'd had hundreds of different jobs in the last twenty five years and none of them had got me anywhere. Croc attacks, failed romance, ruthless bosses.

I was in full flight charging along nicely, beer in hand,

tonsils rattling away when this bloke pulled me aside and introduced himself. He was a professional writer by the name of David Harris, and in all seriousness pointed out that if I could document these experiences down people might really enjoy the read.

Well that was it. As those words left his lips they burned, and I felt like someone living inside my head just pulled on a bit of cord, and a 100-watt globe burst into light. David spoke in earnest, and I found myself compelled to listen.

Was it time to finally make something of myself?

All those years drifting aimlessly around the outback.

Had 'fate' finally caught up with me?

I decided then and there I'd become a writer.

After all I'd tried just about every other profession in life.

There I was one week later perched up on me card table at Waterfall Creek campground in Kakadu National Park pen in hand staring at my writing pad. I'd been trying for three days and three nights and the only thing that had hit the page was about three litres of my sweat.

I'd stumbled straight into a serious writers block, and not only that, it was hot enough to melt the ball-bag off Michelangelo's statue of 'David'. I knew the bestseller was out there, but why wasn't it transmitting?

Maybe it was. But maybe it tried to come through all at once and jammed. I suppose that was technically possible.

No use trying to analyse the rhymes or reasons of a rogue bestseller I thought to myself. If it were that easy every mug would be writing them.

The thing is, when you've turned yourself into a professional writer and you're at your respective card table waiting for that bestseller to channel through, you tend to look around a lot. It's quite common.

Now; camped not far from me was a really interesting young couple. The woman was tall, blonde and exceptionally striking to say the least; she looked like she had a bit of Viking in her. The bloke on the other hand was short, dark, and nuggetty and didn't appear to have come from real good stock at all. His eyebrow began above his left eye and took up most his forehead.

His beard started just under his eyes, went down across his face and neck, spread out across his chest, swung around and went up his back, come back down his chest again and disappeared into his shorts, and from there it could have gone anywhere. In the distance he looked like a Koala that had been burnt in a bushfire.

They really did seem to be an odd couple, but that wasn't any of my business, I had writers block from hell and I was sweating that much I was starting to foam up like an old Draught-horse.

I suppose frustration and the humidity finally got the better of me so I disconnected meself from the card table and headed off down the track to the waterfall, in search of inspiration. The full moon was just coming up and the last few rays of the sunset were gently slipping away. If you can't write a bestseller in a beautiful place like this you mose well give the game away.

Fair dinkum, once I finally crank up I'll probably write two or three of them. Just gotta loosen up.

The waterfall wasn't flowing much, that was to be expected

this time of year, but the billabong looked picturesque with the moonlight flooding across its deep cool stillness.

Though the sun was down by now you still could have boiled an egg in the pocket of your shorts I'm thinkin, as I sat on the sand staring out at the water, waiting for inspiration to find me. Then I heard a rustle in the bush and some footsteps and looked around, and there she was - the 'Blonde Bombshell' from the campground, and she was minus the hairy bloke.

Inspiration had just found me.

The waterfall gently sung its trickling songs as the moonlight lit up the billabong with its luscious silver rays.

We started chatting a bit, her English wasn't too bad and she spoke with a real slow husky Scandinavian type accent and you didn't have to be president of the 'Abba' fan club to work out this woman was Nordic - and she was one hot looking potato.

All of a sudden writers block wasn't an issue.

The conversation mainly revolved around how beautiful the outback is and how lucky we are in this country to be so close to the nature, sentiments I genuinely shared with her. She also pointed out that the bloke back there in the campground was just a friend sharing the fuel expenses. Well... before I even had time to digest that bit of important information, she stripped off, dived into the water, and started breast stroking.

Was this a dream? Was this really happening? Was there really a naked Scandinavian in the billabong?

I had to think about it for a while, probably about point eight of a second and in a blur of desert boots and shorts I was in the drink and breast stroking like a person that had been breast stroking all his life. She had about fifty metres head start but I roared up behind her like 'Flipper', the friendly dolphin.

I know this situation sounds surreal, but when you think about it people that come here after living in the bustle of a European lifestyle, I think get swept away by the beauty and freedom of Australia and just let their hair down. Good on em, I reckon.

Then it suddenly hit me!

Her naked white buttocks sliding through the water with the full moon reflecting off them looked exactly like two Silver Bream swimming along, and mine would have looked like two slightly bigger ones.

Now, I know there were no Saltwater Crocs in that spot but there were plenty of Freshwater Crocs and it's common knowledge they like to hunt at night. Freshhies are generally non aggressive but the night-time was their time, and a Silver Bream was a Silver Bream.

I was seriously wondering just how good their eyesight actually was. We'd breast stroked into what could well have been a very dangerous situation. She was totally oblivious to the fact at any minute her cheeks could be mistakenly chomped. I should have bloody known better, you just don't mess with crocs no matter what type they are.

I could hear them sliding in off the rocks, and I was sure it was gunna be on for young and old, the word was probably out; 'Silver bream in the billabong ... let's get em!'

Something brushed past me and I immediately passed wind and propelled meself forward. Was that a log or what? Shadows were taking on shapes as we reached the waterfall. I was really getting nervous but clinging to the thought: what's a little danger if its gunna lead to romance?

She was yodelling away about how beautiful this place was, no doubt she'd change her tune if something locked onto her glowing white arse cheeks.

We turned for home.

It was a nerve wracking 100 metres but we made it back to the sandy beach both in one piece. My gut feeling told me we'd been watched the whole way. I felt luck was on my side again, as we stood there naked in the moonlight, water beading on her silky brown, voluptuous curves.

Now that the danger was past, I could feel the passion starting to rise. It was just her and me.

She beamed with excitement for the Aussie outback, and I expressed mine in a slightly different way, and by now there was definitely no hiding it.

I'd cracked a fairly substantial erection.

I realize it probably wasn't the politically correct thing to do, but it just reared up. Coincidently, it was about then she decided to make known that she'd been in a relationship with this other woman back home for eight years, and they were kind of married.

'Oh that's great'... I forced out through clenched teeth.

Not really wanting to believe she just said that.

She put her gear on and took off leaving me to ponder the fact that in a very short space of time I'd gone from terror to total embarrassment. I suppose that's what being a professional writer is all about, throwing yourself into challenging situations - expressing yourself.

How was I supposed to know she was bloody gay?

Anyway no harm done I'm thinkin, as I slipped the old shorts and desert boots back on and headed back down the track in the direction of the card table.

Now, this is where the theory of the 'Minor Success' comes into it; O.K. it wasn't a Major Success because unfortunately things didn't pan out the way I would have liked, but in a twist, the anguish I suffered from that little interlude with the 'Nordic Mama' must have helped free up my creative juices, because when I got back and aimed that biro at the page I wrote like there was no tomorrow, and that in itself was a Minor Success.

I wrote about the past, I wrote about the future, I wrote about failed romance and about crazy horses. I wrote about twenty-five hard years on the road and friends made and memories stowed away.

I wrote about steak sandwiches and life, and it felt good to finally get it all out. The writer's block had lifted like an early morning mist and I was goin me hardest.

I really enjoyed writing, it seemed to help me make sense of a lot of things that had happened over the years, and all of a sudden my life took on direction, and that was something I'd been lacking for a long - long time.

Next morning first light found the campground enjoying a little relative cool but anyone with their arse pointing to the ground knew it would heat up once the sun came over the hill. Give it a few hours and it would be like hell with its mouth open.

I pulled up a little groggy after writing well into the night, then drinking even further into the night. By the time I hit the swag I don't think there was much night left.

The early morning fire with its sweet smelling smoke tried its hardest to revive me as I boiled up me Billy and threw in a handful of coffee grounds and some sugar, it was gunna be a serious brew. With a tin of Tom Pipers Irish stew warming up on the edge of the fire breakfast was taking shape.

Across the campground the 'Nordic breast stroking women's favourite' was poking around her camp. She was wrapped up in a pretty little white Sarong and her hair swung shaggily from left to right as she quick stepped it around the Ford Falcon station wagon.

A nearby dome tent quivered and out emerged her friend the hairy bloke; he was wearing green jockettes and a green t-shirt, looking like the Loch Ness Monster's lovechild.

After a scratch of the plums and a rub of the eyes he ferreted out a box of Weet-Bix from the back of the Ford Falcon, but more importantly, his travelling companion dropped her sarong and slid on a pair of shorts and a singlet, not that I was staring or anything.

The coffee started to enter my bloodstream giving me a much-needed lift so I saddled up on me card table, pen in hand, and chipped away at another chapter. I was feeling a little melancholy so I wrote a recollection of love gone wrong.

A few years back I'd had a thing with this Maori girl and she thought I was o.k. as well. It all came to a head the night she invited me around to her farmhouse for a romantic dinner, I rocked up half cut and vomited in her kitchen sink, and she never spoke to me again.

I'd had that one bottled up inside me for years, so writing it down was like therapy. A very sensitive chapter I'm thinkin, as the Ford Falcon idled past.

The sexy blonde apple strudel was driving with the hairy bloke sitting up in the passenger seat, chunks of breakfast cereal embedded into his beard. She smiled and I gave them a wave, they were moving on by the looks.

Were we just ships in the night?

Or was that chance meeting at the billabong just another small piece in the jigsaw of life's fateful interludes?

First David Harris the professional writer sowing the seed at that party, 'Write a book, you can do it', he urged, but it didn't come easy and I almost stumbled and fell, till she came along and picked me up.

Oh well...

I wondered if she'd ever realize just how much she and her glowing white rump helped kick off my writing career. Those arse cheeks really were an integral part of the creative process, and they sure did draw out some emotion. Whichever way you looked at it - I was bestseller bound, and I had her to thank for it.

I stayed on for a few more days at that campground till me supplies started to run a bit low then headed off about 40 kilometres up the track to Mary River Roadhouse. The couple that ran the place was always very hospitable and great fun to catch up with, I usually stopped there a day or two when I

The humble beginnings of a bestseller

was in the area. The result was always the same, a massive hangover and a steak burger with the lot hangin off me ribs.

From there I thought I might drift south for a while, still focused on me best seller but realizing I had to pick up some work soon as there wasn't much honey left in the honey pot.

I steered the old Toyota the 150 kilometres down to the town of Katherine at me usual cruising speed of 80 km an hour. It's probably a little slow but you can relax at that speed and enjoy the trip, give yourself a chance to mull things over a bit.

Katherine was very layback in the afternoon heat; I think everyone was tucked away in pubs and clubs just keeping their fluid levels up. The only movement was a road train grunting its way down the main drag.

I checked out the town's notice board as I usually do just to see what was doing... 'MANGO PICKERS WANTED URGENTLY'.

Well, this came as no surprise.

Every year around this time it's always the same. I'm broke and the only obvious job around is mango picking and I go through the same mental process each time. Basically my brain says 'Go just do it and get a few pay packets together'. Then my self esteem points out to my brain that I've done just about every shit job known to man and the only one I haven't done is mango picking.

So if I weaken and do that, it means I've now done every single shit job, not just most of them - but all of them.

It was a pride thing, if I pick mangoes it means I've finally crossed the line, I'd be Phil O'Brien the bloke that's done every shit job.

The conclusion each year was always the same...

'Fuck the mangoes'.

Another 100kms south and I was driving into down town Mataranka, population 200 - including cattle.

If ever I was going to settle down, which I doubt, I think it might be around Mataranka, they're a good bunch that live there and the town's got everything a bloke needs to survive - diesel, grog and friendly people.

However, there's more to Mataranka than meets the eye, any unsuspecting traveller might just drive straight past this quaint little town and never get to taste her delights. Mataranka harbours a treasure, something that brings tears to a hungry man's eyes.

A warm beefy chunk of paradise.

A Kelly's Pie was a work of art and a thing of rare sculptured beauty. A Kelly's Pie consisted of as much Cow as humanly possible jammed in between crispy layers of pastry. If you ate one on a Monday, you didn't have to eat anything again till Thursday afternoon. Eight times bigger than any other pie in the world the Kelly's Pie was a monument to a great lady Kelly Bryant. Kelly and her partner ran the pub and the roadhouse.

After a short yarn, Kelly reckoned she needed someone to do some yardy work around the pub. With the option of mango picking still fresh in my mind this was a welcome bit of luck.

Being a yardy at a pub revolves around cleaning the beer garden areas, hosing down, stacking fridges and other odd jobs and of course cleaning the toilets. The job wasn't quite rocket science and I thought it might be a good chance to earn a few dollars and think about me bestseller at the same time, maybe cook up a few chapters.

Three days down the track I was really struggling, things weren't panning out the way I'd hoped. I was finding it very hard to face those toilets each day, maybe I was getting soft but a bloke needed nerves of steel. There was more flora and fauna in those toilets than what was roaming the Serengeti plains of Africa.

They were an Alfred Hitchcock horror movie multiplied by ten. I was a professional writer and cleaning those 'shitters' was interfering with the creative process.

I was seriously assessing the situation during a hosing down session out the front of the pub, when a pommy backpacker walked past. He was down on his luck, no money he reckoned, and he couldn't find a job.

'You'll be right mate' I told him ... 'you can have mine'.

So I handed him the hose and that was that.

'No long service owing on that one' I was thinking as I headed east up the Roper Highway at 80 kph.

This is pretty well how my life had been for many years, drifting, restless, answering to no-one and going nowhere, and just like Frank Sinatra, I did it my way, but things were different now, I was on a mission, a quest, in search of that mysterious bestseller.

I had a duty and a responsibility to the lovers of fine literature to bring this one home. Drinking large amounts of grog and going from job to job wasn't gunna get it done.

I needed to focus.

The Roper Highway was taking me deep into the Roper Valley, home to the mighty Roper River. This was Top End cattle country; hard, merciless, tough and unforgiving - and that was on a good day.

Some say the Roper Valley is the arsehole of the world, well if that's true Big River station was 220 km fair up it.

It took a big man to tame that country, a man like Daniel Tapp, he'd ride anything wrapped in fur, especially after a six-pack, and he ate anything that ate grass.

Well respected by his piers, Daniel was a bloody good bloke, and the type of stockman Slim Dusty sang about for so many years. I'd met him a few years earlier in a stock camp at Macarthur River, he was head stockman there and possessed a bunch of really good horses. Nothing ever got past him when he was mustering, if a beast tried he'd throw it, castrate it, roll a smoke and be back on his horse while other people were still thinking about it.

I really admired Daniel and I'd been meaning to catch up with him for a long time.

The track leading into Big River station was pretty rough and ready as I wound my way through the scrub, and then out onto an anthill studded valley...fat cattle everywhere.

Up on the hill overlooking the valley was the Big River Homestead. The homestead was actually a large shed which included inside its four corrugated iron walls - several stripped down vehicles, a truck, a caravan, every tool known to man, pipes, saddles, a wife, fishing gear, guns, a kitchen sink, barb wire, hay and a large pack of wild looking working dogs.

This was the nerve centre.

The handshake was warm and welcoming - 'Couldn't have blown in at a better bloody time', Daniel reckoned, in his usual happy go lucky drawl.

He was opening up a bit of new country and had a lot of fencing to put up.

Living there with him was his wife Shannon, she could work as hard as him but she was just a whole heap better looking.

Weeks fell off the calendar as the three of us got stuck into it. Working with Daniel and Shannon was one of those really enjoyable stints a bloke drops into from time to time. All the

Beef and Barramundi you could eat, good company and a nice pay cheque at the end of it. I suppose I stayed about a month before the wet season started to set in and the fencing was wrapped up.

No doubt I'd get back there another day, but a month at Big River Station had left me inspired and I had chapters flyin out of me left right and centre.

Camped in the bush back near Mataranka I piloted the card table through another chapter, a gruelling recollection about these three Japanese girls I took on a four-day trip to Kakadu when I was working as a tour guide a while ago. A slight mis-understanding took place - thinking it was a dead set goer, I tried to kiss one of them on the first night.

I thought I was in like Flynn. I thought she was sugared up. Big mistake.

I'd read it all wrong.

She was just being polite like most Japanese people are and I interpreted it as a bit of a green light. They didn't talk to me again for the next three days and nights of the tour. You could have cut the air with a knife. Then when I dropped them off back in Darwin, they all reckoned 'Sayonara', which I'm pretty sure means piss off in Japanese.

That was just more emotional baggage I had been harbour-ing and now it could be finally released onto the page. I hope that taking all the guilt I felt with it.

I lost myself for the next few weeks, just driving a bit, writing a bit and camping out in all sorts of places. Drifting south, away from the tropics and the wet season, creeping deeper in-side myself, and dragging out stuff from the past, stuff that needed to be written down and dealt with.

Daniel Tapp

Why had I had hundreds of different jobs and gone nowhere? Or had I? Maybe cruising along at 80 kph with the sunlight filtering through the windscreen was somewhere? Maybe this is the best place to be, and the other 22 million people in Australia have got it wrong? Was that possible?

Highly bloody unlikely, but what a great theory.

Still the same, it was all food for thought and thinking was something I was doing a lot of these days. I've always been a great believer that a bloke doesn't have to go to Tibet and sip goat's milk with a monk for six months to get the answers, the answers are there all the time, and you just got to learn to access them. Staring deeply into a steak burger with the lot at Aileron roadhouse, it came to me.

I let my mind wander for a bit and I saw myself standing at

a crossroad, and on one side I could see an old raggedy looking swag spread out on the dirt surrounded by empty beer cans and hordes of blowflies. Up the track on the other side of the crossroads, was a brand new four wheel drive parked out the front of a flash looking air conditioned library, and people were gathering for a book launch.

The vision faded and once again I was staring back at a humble steak burger.

There was no doubt about it, I'd come to the time in my life where I needed to make some real decisions and steer a course for the future.

Up until now, most of my big decisions centred on where to get the next tank of diesel? Or whether to try and crack on to the barmaid at closing time?

I was in my thirties and I knew deep down I wasn't being premature in thinking it was time to raise the bar a bit. It was time to do something completely out of character, something so far fetched it was bordering on the ridiculous.

I was going to actually 'save' the money I had left over from the Big River Station job and try to pick up some more work and really build up my finances. Now for a bloke like me, that was a bizarre concept, but as crazy as it sounded... it just might work. After all I was a professional writer with a best seller riding on me back. People in the literary world were probably already talking about this book and the impact it was gunna have on society. With their literary sixth sense they could probably feel a big one was coming up; just like me they could probably smell it.

Now that I was a born again responsible money saver I wasn't about to let them down either, I was gunna bring home the bacon - page by page

Another beautiful morning in Central Australia the 'Red

Heart,' not a cloud in the sky. A gentle breeze caressed my early morning fire sending the Billy into a quick frenzied boil. Today was the first day of the rest of my life and I wanted it to be something really bloody special. I was hoping the red heart of Australia could pump some employment out of one of its arteries.

After a gourmet breakfast consisting of strong black coffee and a tin of Heinz baked beans in ham sauce I was gassed up ready to take on the world. My strategy was to roll into Alice Springs around lunchtime and see if I could sniff out some work. Best place to start was probably the pub I thought, I'll just see who's around and hopefully get my finger on the pulse. Shouldn't take too long to hear of a bit of work going someplace.

Several hours after strolling into the pub full of purpose, I staggered out, full of piss, and curled up in the front seat of the Toyota.

The first day of the rest of my life hadn't quite panned out the way I planned... actually it wasn't real pretty at all. No chapters got written, no money got saved and no jobs were got.

I woke up about 4am the following morning feeling like something furry that had just been hit by a road train. It took me till about 4.17am to actually work out where I was, and how I got there.

Nothing like a night contorted around the gear stick of a four-wheel drive to keep a bloke honest. I never realized being a professional writer could be so physically demanding.

I stuck to my guns and after surviving one of the worst hangovers endured by man in the past millennium, I was back on the hunt for some employment.

I wore out some boot leather over the next few days but it

was worth it because I came across what appeared to be a pretty good little number.

A tour company needed a driver come guide to fill in for a few weeks. They specialized in a shuttle type service between Alice and Darwin so if you were a tourist and wanted an alternative to flying or coach travel you could go with this mob and take a few days and see a bit of country and enjoy the journey.

They reckoned I was just the bloke they were looking for.

Getting the job driving for the tourist shuttle bus mob was a timely stroke of luck, and that's all I needed, a little luck. At last there seemed to be some light at the end of the literary tunnel.

So feeling a little more relaxed with the way things were going, I pumped out a chapter. I let myself reflect on days gone by when I attempted to start my own particular tourism venture, 'Phil O'Brien Safaris.'

I went broke after one trip.

It was a harsh reflection of my financial capabilities but all the same I felt people might enjoy the read, and it will probably make them feel better about their own financial positions. That's what this bestseller is all about I was thinkin, making people feel good about themselves.

And you didn't have to be head astronomer at the Mount Stromlo Observatory to work out I was bloody focused!

There's gunna be more well meaning philosophy in this book than you can poke a stick at, I'll probably have the Dalai Llama ringing me up for tips, I'm thinkin.

So onwards and upwards I soared, I was Mel Gibson leading from the front in 'Braveheart', I was 'Phar Lap' running home strong in the cup, I was 'The Don' flicking one off his toes for four. I was all these things rolled into one positive chunk of human flesh. I was well on the way to achieve what I'd set out to achieve – I was unstoppable.

The thunderclouds built as I headed north in the shuttle bus with my cargo of ten rowdy backpackers. It did feel a little strange heading north again, especially after me plan all along was to head south. But going in the wrong direction was something I was used of doing and besides, it was for the cause, it was all for the cause.

Darwin was well into the grips of the wet season when we shuttled in three days after leaving the Alice. It was a pretty good trip, the backpackers were interested in most of the stuff I showed them, and the 1,500 kilometres were traversed in good spirits. We said our goodbyes in Darwin and after a day off I picked up about eight new backpackers for the trip back down to Alice Springs.

We shuttled out of the wet season and back down to the hot clear summery heat of the Red Centre. It was another good trip with a nice bunch of travellers from around the globe, three days on the road, everyone happy, not a problem.

After dropping them off at their various accommodations in Alice Springs I headed for the depot, hopefully to jag another trip and also collect me whopping pay packet. This mob will look after me, I was thinking. Once the good reports come flooding in from the backpackers the company will probably want to give me a bonus and beg me to stay on.

Well... The apologies came thick and fast from the bloke running the show.

'We thought we could hang on', he reckoned 'Things just got too tight'.

Too tight? What's this bloke talking about?

'We're closing the doors'.

'Closing what doors?' I asked him, trying to fathom where

this conversation was actually heading.

'We've gone bust... 'Kaput', we can't afford to honour any of our debts - the show's over'.

All of a sudden it became clear to me what this bloke was saying... I think it went something along the lines of - 'I aint getting paid'!!

I felt like trying to choke the money out of him but I could see by the hang dog look on his face the situation was serious, what ever way you looked at it, there was gunna be no pot of gold at the end of this rainbow, and I was really counting on that money.

A wave of depression splashed over me as I moped off down the road feeling lower than a black snake's arse.

Phil O'Brien formally known as 'unstoppable' had just come to a grinding screeching halt.

The thing is if it was just me drifting aimlessly around it wouldn't really matter but it's like when you've got a wife, you've gotta at least feed her and make her happy, it's a commitment. Well, it was the same for me; I was committed in my mind and my heart to finish this book.

It wasn't just me anymore, my life was bigger than that now, and just because the going gets a bit tough a bloke just can't walk away from something he's committed to.

But I tell you what, I'd dropped me bundle.

I tried to do some writing later that day but it just wasn't coming out, I was creatively constipated, and the ink just wasn't flowing. I was wound up tighter than a Swiss Watch maker's favourite watch.

So my commitment and me packed up and left Alice Springs, no point hangin around - the bubble had burst.

Eighty kilometres south of the Alice I called into 'Jim's

Place' a great little roadside stop run by an old family friend Jim Cottrell. Jim was in good form and he introduced me to his pet dingo 'Dinky'.

The dingo kept jumping up on the old piano Jim had in the corner. He'd press on the keys with his paws and howl in tune. Jim explained he was proving a big hit with the tourists. I'm thinkin', the dingo probably had as much chance of writing a best seller as I did.

With Dinky crooning away in the background Jim and me yarned a bit and he reckoned he'd definitely buy some books from me when I'd finished it.

When - and if, I told Jim.

When - and if?

I collected a few more kilometres in the old Toyota that day and wondered if I'd made the right moves of late. Perhaps I would have been better off picking mangoes back up in Katherine, or with my arm shoved down the 'S' bend unblocking the toilets at Mataranka Pub? By now the pay packets would have been adding up, but would the chapters be getting written, that was the big one.

My life was really just a support system for the best seller.

I was just the antenna that it happened to be channelling through.

It was all a question of balance, could I keep it all together, stay on track write the big one and just keep the cogs turning?

It was all a question of balance.

Not getting paid for that last job definitely unbalanced the whole show. Psychologically I had the wobbles. Self-pity, writers block, life was about as balanced as a magpie goose that had just been shot through one wing. I felt like I'd stumbled into the black hole of Calcutta without a torch.

So I did what I normally do when life's dilemmas build up a little too much, I pulled into the next roadhouse for a beer.

Erldunda was a real hive of activity in the late afternoon.

Busses pulling in after their tours from Uluru, Aboriginal families fuelling up for their trip back out to where-ever, and a few stockman and tourists looking to quench their thirst.

Erldunda was a remote transit point for all types of people going to all types of places, and I was probably the only one there, that was going nowhere.

I had 'Destination Unknown' written across me forehead as I did a slow march to the bar. With beer in hand I sat there pretty down and out, having a good old ponder, then, through the juke box distortion I heard a voice from alongside me, it was a voice that I'd heard before and I half recognized it, but I couldn't quite place it.

I turned around and there she was... ravishing... wild platinum locks draped shaggily over her rustic Nordic beauty.

Well I'll be buggered.

It was the bombshell from the billabong a couple of months back. She gently let her turquoise eyes meet with my blood-shot blues and in a husky Scandinavian smoulder, she quietly spoke. That night swimming naked in the moonlight was something she'd never ever forget she told me, and it will always be a cherished memory of her trip to the outback.

If only she knew how that night had impacted on me as well, but I couldn't really speak, my heart was jammed up in me throat.

What a shame she was batting for the other team, I was thinkin. She purred away about her trip to Uluru and it was so nice to run into her again and for the moment I just let my gaze rest on her warm sunny smile.

This girl had saved me from the dreaded writers block once before right back at the beginning of my quest to write the best seller, her nakedness sliding through that moonlit billabong had really jerked free some emotion, and with each word she spoke, once again I could feel my spirits lifting above this gloomy period I was going through.

This was a signal, the timing of our chance meeting was no coincidence, this was Divine Intervention, and you didn't need Pope Paul the 5th to sign off on that one.

Was that a choir of angels I could hear?

No, it was just the 'Dixie Chicks' taking their turn on the jukebox, but all the same I felt like maybe I was getting some guidance from above. This thing was getting way bigger than just me and the Toyota driving around the bush trying to write a book... it was gettin' spiritual.

I thought I better validate that with another beer when the toilet door opened behind her and out emerged her travelling companion, the hairy bloke. He'd trimmed himself up a bit but he still looked like a walking talking five o'clock shadow.

We had a few quiet ones together and settled into each other's company for a while, just yarning it up. The night slipped on and it got to the stage where it was time for them to go, so I walked out as well.

Looking down I couldn't help but notice her left and right buttocks were more out of her shorts than in; it was like I was saying G'day to two old friends. Just before she climbed in the Ford Falcon station wagon she looked at me and said 'I hope you get to where ever you're going' and we gently shook hands.

It was as if she knew what I'd been going through.

They pulled out and headed north, the hairy bloke sitting up in the passenger seat like one of those cement Mexicans people have in their gardens.

A couple of hours ago I could have easily thrown the towel in on this crusade I was on, but a kind word from a kind soul got me once again on the right track. I never did catch her name either, I was thinkin, as I headed south to the one horse border town of Kulgera.

I was so inspired I sunk half a dozen in record time, set up camp, and wrote a fabulous chapter.

I woke before the sun and with the light from the morning star I managed to scrape up enough wood to boil a much needed Billy. My first waking thought that morning was of the Danish Angel, I was so fiercely attracted to her I ached, but I knew that it was just a waste of time daydreaming, she was gay and she was heading north, I was broke and heading south.

Even an eternal optimist like me couldn't find a solution to that one.

Although I'd never forget her, it wasn't gunna get me anywhere so I decided to just let it go for now and concentrate on the job at hand, which was - making a really strong coffee.

'Sparrow fart' is my favourite part of the day; I love all the things that happen at that time, the coolness in the air, and the colours on the horizon, the bird songs and the feeling of anticipation mixed up in the serenity.

A bloke can meditate on what lays ahead, and I've always cooked up my best plans staring into a fire before sun up.

It was gunna be tight, but if I didn't eat or drink too much I'd make it down to Adelaide, about 1200 kilometres away.

Adelaide was the most realistic place to base myself for a while. My mum lived there so I had a place to camp, also my sister wasn't far away and she was a pretty handy typist in her day so hopefully we could team up.

I crossed the border into South Australia mid morning feeling pretty bloody optimistic.

I liked S.A, I felt I had a bit of an affinity with the place, as that's where I went to school and have spent some time there by and by. Unfortunately it always seemed a lot harder to drop in to a bit of work there. It was way more formal than the Northern Territory and people always asked for references and a 'curriculum vitae'.

I'd never bothered much with references, and 'curriculum vitae' sounded like a Portuguese breakfast cereal.

Whatever it was, I didn't have one.

So I just kept on moving and burning ink wherever I got the urge. The stories and the recollections flowed easy on that leg of the literary journey. 'Marla', 'Cagney', and 'Coober Pedy' the open sparseness of the bush there and the desolation really agreed with me. Starry nights, red raw sunrises, the Mid North had a good flavour and it's what I call honest country.

Sunset overlooking the salt lakes near Pimba is something that will stay with me for a long time, the myriad of soft colours making up the sunset and their reflections on the stark pale endlessness of the dried salt flats, really was a sight.

I liked Pimba; Pimba was my type of town, surrounded by miles of nothing life revolved around 'Spuds 24 Hour', which was pretty well the town.

It's an uncomplicated place and just down the road is the Woomera Rocket Range, which is handy if you ever needed to launch a rocket.

It was all just so convenient.

If I wasn't so broke I would have liked to hang around there

Destination: Bestseller

a bit longer, but I did manage to write a few choice pages.

After a few cold ones on a salt flat I decided the book was pretty well near completion. I'd jammed about as much of my soul in there as I possibly could, and as I looked at the bits of paper spilling out of the plastic 'Woolies' shopping bag I felt a bit of emotion.

This wasn't just a pile of paper shoved in a plastic bag. This humble bag contained my life, the good the bad and the ugly.

Next morning I packed up camp, no more starry nights, and no more reflections by the campfire, no more meanderings; it was onwards to the city of Adelaide...destination bestseller.

I blew through Port Augusta in a trance, a steak burger with the lot at Port Wakefield and before I knew it I was winding through the suburban streets of Adelaide the 'City of

Churches'.

Once again it was a bit moving I suppose. It had been a fairly intense last couple of months on the road and I hadn't had it all me own way either.

But now it was all in front of me.

I knew nothing about publishing a book, but that wasn't gunna stop me, lack of knowledge never stopped me doing anything in the past, and it wasn't gunna stop me now. I'd have this one out of the plastic bag and in the shops in no time I was thinkin, as I pulled into my mums driveway with the fuel gauge firmly planted on 'E', which contrary to public opinion doesn't stand for 'Empty'.

It stands for... 'Enough'.

Sir Charles Kingsford Smith couldn't have come home on a wing and a prayer any better than what I did.

I was flat stony broke ... but geez I had potential.

As I disembarked the old road weary Toyota I was greeted by my mum who promptly asked that age old question mothers have been asking their sons for thousands of years.

'Have you got a bloody job yet'?

I told her I was working as a professional writer.

'What's that pay'? She reckoned.

Well, its one of those jobs where you have to give and take a bit. At the moment I'm at the part where you just give.

'O.K Earnest Hemingway, give me those rags off your back and I'll give them a birthday and throw them in the washing machine'.

Obviously my mum was taking my newfound artistic direction quite seriously. When I presented my sister with a plastic bag full of bits of paper and asked her if she could type it up, I think she soon realized she was gunna be involved in something pretty major.

'Are you fricken kidding!' She said... with volume.

I explained there'd been a lot of great crusades through history, but nothing quite like the one I was on, there was more twists and turns here than two snakes having sex on a rocky ridge.

So over the next few weeks and a bit more persuasion my sister came good and hit some form with the word processor, her fingers tap dancing across the keypad, although she found it a bit hard to deal with the fact that all the stories were - unfortunately true.

To her credit she stuck to the task and the chapters started to take shape.

I scored a bit of work picking grapes up at this vineyard in the Adelaide Hills. I couldn't believe it, an actual job in Adelaide that didn't require fifteen references from past employers. Then I worked out why.

It was a beautiful setting and they were lovely people but you only got paid for what you picked. I think it was a dollar a bucket, and there was a real knack to it. Some wiry skinny little blokes were doing O.K. getting in and under the vines, snipping away. I don't think I ever made more than thirty dollars a day myself, probably due to the fact I was putting more time in trying to pick up one of the female pickers than actually doing any real grape picking.

I didn't do any good there either. But it was a break from life on the road.

I'd got into a pretty nice routine there for a while in Adelaide, things like not having to collect firewood every time you wanted a cup of coffee, no ants in the swag, and not having to worry about where you were gunna roll it out each night. I caught up with a bit of sport on T.V and of course the latest news and current affairs programs, of which there's numerous.

The current affair shows I found quite fascinating, each channel had their own, and each night the three main topics were always the same – a crooked builder running amuck building dodgy houses in the suburbs, followed by an obesity story, and then they'd always wop in a really down and out 'tear jerker' story, about some old age pensioner having to eat canned dog food because they had no money left.

It was funny, every show was the same, but no one really noticed. Anyway, I'd give them something new to talk about when me best seller blasts into their lives, that'll give them something to put in their pipes and smoke, I was thinkin, as I urged me sister to type faster.

Now, just when you finally think everything is going along quite nicely and success is staring you in the face, the wheels fall off, and even an experienced professional writer like me never saw it coming.

You see it all came to a head when all the stuff had finally been typed up by my sister, all the bits of paper, stuff on the back of beer coasters and scribbles on toilet paper. It had all been compiled and typed, but which ever way you looked at it there just wasn't enough material there to fill up a book. My handwriting was quite big so it was deceiving; once it was typed there just wasn't the volume. There was no way around it I had to dig deep and go back inside myself and drag out some more chapters

Life wasn't meant to be easy, not mine anyway.

It just goes to show you, don't count your best sellers before they hatch.

I handed in me snippers at the vineyard and I told the girl I'd been chasing for weeks that she could have had me, if she played her cards right. It was like water off a ducks back as she spat out seeds from a grape she'd been sucking on.

Fair enough, I wasn't hangin around anyway.

Nice people - picking nice grapes - in nice locations.

It was all very nice.

But it wasn't nice enough.

I had three quarters of a best seller, and that was worth five eights of stuff all, if I didn't get it finished.

It was time to load up the Toyota for one last effort. No point trying to write in the suburbs I knew I just couldn't do that, I needed space around me. I was in a bit of a predicament because as nice as grape picking had been, I'd made bugger all money.

My brother in law came to the rescue and lent me quite a substantial amount of hoot from a long service payout he got from the place he'd been working for many years. It was an incredibly generous act especially due to the fact neither one of us knew how I was going to pay it back, but I was mobile again.

I drove north through the farms and gently rolling hills, dairies and vineyards, and down main streets running through quaint towns. It was all very charming but I didn't feel a connection so I kept travelling letting my sixth sense make the decisions. About four hours north of Adelaide I found the place I needed, the beautiful rugged 'Flinders Ranges'.

The panoramas were rich and spectacular and I could really feel the spirit there. There was no doubt in my mind the beauty and the solitude of the Flinders was all I needed to jerk a few more stories out of the depths of my soul and set this book free.

So for forty days and forty nights I wandered, and as far as I know that's only been done one other time in history, also by a man that was very passionate about his beliefs.

Uphill and along stony creek beds I walked writing pad in hand, chapters flowing out like lava, biro-spitting ink like a machine gun, I wasn't holding back, I wasn't taking any prisoners.

I got personal.

I wrote about adventure - I wrote about the time I worked as a Crocodile Farmer without any actual knowledge of Crocodiles. I wrote about being a Mackerel Fisherman, without any real knowledge of Mackerel. I wrote about being a Drink Waiter and getting fired after only 27 seconds on the job. I wrote about singing a song to a bunch of German tourists around a campfire, and their horrified response as my left testicle dropped out the side of my shorts mid song.

Did the world really need to know that?

Possibly not.

But it was going in the book - just in case.

I hadn't had all these hundreds of jobs and experiences for nothing, all these things had happened for a reason, I'd been on a road, a pathway through life that had taken me to the place I am now.

As I looked up at the stars burning fiercely over the Hawker Hotel car park I could finally see this journeys end was just around the corner. From the testing humidity of the Top End - to the parched Red Centre, then onto the panoramic inspiration of the Flinders Ranges. I've had to expect the unexpected, just like those interludes with that mysterious but beautiful Danish woman that always turned up just when all hope seemed lost. Or that time I stared into a steak burger with the lot at Aileron roadhouse and saw my future. I thought that was only meant to happen with 'Crystal Balls'?

My life had become anything but normal, not that it ever was to start with.

A shooting star blazed its way across a phosphorus sky lit with jewels, snapping me out of the moment, and so I spurred the Toyota on into the crisp cool darkness, and once again the wheels turned, on this literary labour of love.

My pilgrimage to the Flinders had been very successful and the new material I'd written combined really well with the stuff we already had. Failed romance, failed business ventures, and other varied misadventurous failures. Was it my imagination, or was there a theme forming here?

I decided to call the book '101 Adventures that have got me absolutely nowhere', and it was just how I envisaged it would be. Finally, I got the book printed, and for the first time in my life I really felt that I'd achieved something, and just like David Harris predicted, people really did want to read my yarns.

'101 Adventures That Have Got Me Absolutely Nowhere' became a best seller, I couldn't believe it.

People found my gypsy lifestyle really interesting and the whole thing was a complete whopping 'Major' Success.

Well... for a while anyway.

That's how it goes; it was a Major Success to start with, but by the time I paid my brother in law back, and then I paid the Printer, and not to mention the Distributor and a herd of other bills associated with publishing a book. The rip roaring Major Success had to be down graded to just a basic Minor Success.

Actually, all I got out of the whole project was about enough money to buy a Ham and Pineapple Pizza and a can of coke. I was as fucken broke as when I started.

Pardon the French!

THE BIG ACCIDENT

STOOPED AND RIGID - silhouetted against a ruddy red outback horizon. A primeval metallic hulk. The mighty 'Delta 7' stood there in the pre dawn like an aging dinosaur.

Not exactly state of the art, the Delta 7 was one of the oldest drilling rigs in the Wallis Drilling fleet. Mounted on the back of an aged semi trailer the Delta 7 had character.

It was what you call a 'Diamond Drilling Rig'. It used a drill bit encrusted with Industrial diamonds designed to cut through rock. Every metre the Rig drilled down it would produce a core sample of the rock underground, giving the geologist a good look at what was down there, and if there was the potential for a decent gold deposit.

Wallis Drilling Company or 'Wally World' as it was affectionately known to its employees had rigs scattered all around Western Australia from the Kimberleys up north down to Esperance in the south.

Me and the Delta 7 were somewhere in the middle, at a place called German Well.

There was a boom happening. Gold prices were good and mineral exploration was taking place on a large scale. Mining companies were all scrambling for a slice of the action. But there wasn't a lot of action at German Well.

Besides the well itself, there was nothing else around but scrub and more scrub for as far as the eye could see. The nearest town was Meekatharra, which was a good three hour drive. Every couple of weeks one of us would make the trip to pick up supplies which was a real occasion because you'd get to see the odd female, which reassured us that there actually was another sex sharing the planet, and it wasn't just a rumour.

The only other living thing at German Well was a Goanna that used to show up sometimes and make off with me dirty socks.

Apart from him - there was just us.

'Us' was Phil McComish the driller who operated the Delta 7 and me as the faithful offsider, plus a geologist and his team of three blokes. One of the geologist's crew was a big barrel-gutted bloke called Harry. Harry would have weighed in at about 20 stone in the old money, and was your real typical jolly fat bloke.

I don't know if anyone was finding any gold, but we all got on pretty good at German Well, and life just meandered along.

The day of 'The Big Accident' started just like any other day. A quick run around the Delta 7 with the grease gun, check the oil levels, fuel up and then kick her in the guts. After a few moans and groans the old girl would fire up and off we'd go. The Drilling was very slow that morning due to the very hard rock so it gave me a bit of spare time to catch up on this really good novel I'd been reading for the past two weeks. Unfortunately I never got to find out how it ended because Phil McComish had torn the last three pages out for toilet paper when I wasn't around. He apologised and said it was a bit of an emergency. I asked him if he read any of it before he used it. He remembered reading a paragraph but it

Author Phol O'Brien with core sample and the mighty Delta 7 rattling away in the background

wasn't enough for me to piece the ending together. Even though we laughed about it I was a little upset and I suppose the hangover didn't help.

We'd had a few beers the night before because Harry had done a shop run into Meekatharra and came back with a few cartons so we'd downed a couple.

Actually, it was more than just a couple.

Phil McComish had cooked up a really good roast and I'd scoffed into it with so much aggression I ate the bottom out of the paper plate. Later that night I crashed out in me tent and for some reason I missed the pillow, and my head hung off the end of me stretcher bed at a pretty weird angle. As a result I snored that loud one of the other blokes got up in the middle of the night to take a leak but was scared to go out of his tent because he thought there was a mob of feral pigs outside goin' through the camp.

Anyway like I said, the day of the Big Accident started just like any normal day at German Well did - slow and steady.

Lunch time came and as usual me and Phil McComish dined on our usual gourmet delight of Tinned Dog (canned food) heated up on the edge of a camp fire. The Rig rattled on through lunch and we'd just eat as we go. 'Wally World' liked the Rig to be drilling at least 12 hours every day so the only time it stopped was when it broke down, which was reasonably often. The arvo dragged on due to the fact it never broke down, and the slow drilling thanks to the tough bedrock. No one had any idea this was to be the day of the Big Accident, the monotony of German Well was about to be smashed.

I had plenty of time to ponder over the end of the novel I'd wasted two weeks reading. It would have been fine if he'd torn out the acknowledgement section, or the index, but no, he had to go and wipe his arse with the really 'gripping climax'.

But don't get me wrong Phil McComish was a great bloke, and a good mate. He'd not long got over a marriage break up with his first wife. As it panned out him and his wife did what a lot of Aussies do these days. They performed the 'Big Swap'.

The Big Swap is getting really common. Technically it's when you take off with your next-door neighbour's missus and her husband takes off with yours. This is getting so common now it's almost like an Aussie tradition, just like Anzac Day or Boiling the Billy. The Big Swap is just another iconic Aussie thing to do.

Sunset came, and time to put the screaming vibrating rust-

Phil McComish

ing old Delta 7 to rest for the night. Me and Phil just whacked a bit more tinned dog on the coals as we didn't really feel like cookin up a proper feed. Big Harry turned up with three cold ones so we sat around and watched the sunset and unwound a bit.

The time of the Big Accident was drawing near.

Harry reckoned he'd worked out it was Mother's Day today and he'd brewed up this idea to drive over to Gidgee Gold Mine and use their phone and ring our mothers up.

It was a good two hour drive over to Gidgee the little gold mine, but there wasn't anything else to do. Social events at German Well were few and far between so off we went in Harry's Toyota tray back, and to German Well residents, this was a big night out.

It was a pretty cosy fit in the front with Harry taking up most of the room with his twenty stone plus, and Phil McComish and me packed in tight. The day had been hot and steamy and storm clouds were starting to build as we drove into the remains of a beautiful rusty coloured sunset. Everyone was completely oblivious to the impending Big Accident.

We made Gidgee Gold Mine at about 8.30, and me and Phil had a quick G'day to our respective mothers on the phone and then hopped into a few beers with the blokes from Gidgee. While Harry, who enjoyed a yarn, gasbagged to his Mum. About 10 o'clock Harry finally puffs out and gets off the phone and we head for home, back to downtown German Well.

The storm that had been brewing all arvo had let go and there was some serious rain and lightning all around as we ploughed on down the slippery bush track. Treacherous conditions – 'Big Harry' and his 20 stone jammed behind the wheel.

Big Harry reckoned he'd done a lot of rally driving and he could handle any conditions in a four wheel drive. He was an expert, not a problem. Relax; enjoy the trip he reckoned, as he slipped a 'Deep Purple' cassette into the player and his head started jerking forward and back to the hard rock beat.

Down the road we sailed.

A blinding flash of lightning, headlights covered in mud, water on the road, we're going sideways, too fast, and Harry's lost it.

We're out of control...

Aaaaaaahhhh!

The terrible sounds of the Toyota falling apart as the tray back rolled down the isolated bush track. Big Harry's 20 stone bouncing around the cab, 100 kilometres an hour, pulverising me and Phil Mc Comish.

Someone's knee hits the cassette player and Deep Purple gets turned onto full blast. I think the song was called 'Space truckin' and the guitarist launched into a wild guitar solo and we're rolling and crashing and the world's spinning and the guitar screams away on full volume, and Harry's unbridled beef is crushing us to death.

It was just a nightmare.

The Toyota comes to a spine shaking jerk and its over.

We landed back on our wheels and its all dark and I'm in shock and 'Space truckin' is blasting out.

Are we dead? Am I dead? I wasn't sure.

If this was the 'After world' I'm thinkin, someone was playing a really loud electric guitar in it.

I think I blacked out for a minute and I came to again and a lightning flash lit the scene up and I saw Harry running though the scrub like a crazed bullock, and he was yelling out 'I've killed them,' 'I've killed them'.

I looked across at Phil McComish; he was half squashed in between the gap between the front seats. Normally a bloke could never fit into such a small gap, but on this particular occasion he did. He dragged himself out then helped me out and it must have been the shock, but I did a projectile vomit that would have gone the length of a cricket pitch. I'd had a fair few beers at Gidgee and I suppose it was just like when you shake up a bottle of Coke, and then open it, my guts had just been through the same process. Anyway it was probably the longest spew ever performed, and me and Phil couldn't help but burst out laughing, and with Harry still crashing around in the scrub yelling 'I've killed them' and Deep Purple carving up on the cassette player, it all just added to the craziness and a bloke just had to laugh.

Harry did a few more laps then came back sobbing and couldn't believe we made it.

The cassette player finally chewed up Deep Purple and after a few gurgles and one last burst of wild guitar it was just eerie silence.

The three of us just stood there for a while, numb with shock. The storm had moved away but the lightning still lit the place up a bit.

The Toyota was smashed up but it wasn't what you'd think. After a vehicle's rolled you'd expect the panels etc to be bent inwards but in this rollover all the doors and roof was pushed out. Harry's 20 stone of runaway beef had wrecked everything from the inside out. The roof looked like it had been peeled open with a can opener. Either our heads lifted it or else it was Harry ricocheting around that broke all the welds. The doors were bowed right out as well. They weren't dented in they were bowed out. It must have been the first time in the history of car accidents anyone has written a Toyota off... from the inside.

All to the tune of 'Space truckin'.

We never blamed Harry for the 'Big Accident' it could have happened to anyone. The conditions that night were really greasy and it was just bad luck that's all.

So there we are in the middle of the track all still a bit rattled, but now that the shock was wearing off a bit the aches and pains started to reveal themselves. We all were sore as hell and a long way from German Well.

Looking at the vehicle, the tray was smashed, the chassis was twisted, the roof was peeled off, all the glass was gone but to its credit the thing started and we were able to limp back to German Well doin a very wobbly 5 km an hour.

We were very lucky the vehicle made it otherwise it would have been a long night waiting for help on that track, because there wasn't a real lot of traffic heading in the German Well direction.

Next morning I was in a fair bit of pain. I knew I'd done something to my back and so I drove into Meekatharra to see the doctor. I really needed an x-ray but the three hour drive was in vain. The Doctor's x-ray machine was only a small one. It could only x-ray a wrist or an ankle. So he gave me some painkillers and it was back to work. A month or so later I had to throw the towel in; my back just wasn't getting any better. I finally made it back down to Perth and got an x-ray and as I expected one of my discs in the lower part of my back was pretty well crushed.

I was lucky I could get around at all.

My days on the Delta 7 came to an end, and for a while I had to give the heavy lifting a break and let me back recover a bit. It was all pretty sad. I'd really enjoyed the job, and apart from German Well I'd been to some great places around Western Australia with that old Rig.

It was a good life, long days working and even longer nights drinking, and if you were near a town with women in it then you could add womanising to the list as well. It was at times pretty wild, but in an honest Aussie sort of way.

But in the end, the way things panned out turned into a Minor Success, as they somehow seem to do, because one thing led to another and I ended up becoming a Crocodile farmer, which was a much safer occupation.

FLYING FOX DREAMING

I FORGOT ALL ABOUT WHERE I WAS GOING TO OR where I had come from, I was just in the moment. The middle of nowhere, sunset, a six pack and reclining in my favourite old deckchair, no one around for miles, just me and me old Toyota.

A huge colony of flying foxes had taken off from their roost on the banks of the nearby Mainoru River and were blacking out the sky there was so many of them. As they headed out west towards the sunset it was a beautiful sight.

Thousands upon thousands of bats flying into the deep red glow.

Spontaneous - free-searching - mysterious.

A silky black aurora.

I was totally spellbound as I sucked on a can.

It really is the simple things in life that move a bloke the most I'm thinkin, getting a little deep and meaningful.

In my mind I declared this most charming moment in nature a Major Success, and I couldn't believe my luck that I was there to witness it.

A few hours later the colony must have done a 'U-Turn' and decided to head back my way. They screeched and cackled all night in the trees above my camp and shat all over everything.

My deckchair got shat on; the old Toyota got severely shat on and me and me swag copped several direct hits.

So I decided in view of the recent course of events and after some serious consideration that it was probably best for all concerned if I officially downgraded the moment to just a Minor Success.

THE GIRL THAT NEVER RANG

SHE TOLD ME SHE'D RING ME. For sure, no worries, the phone will be ringing any minute now. Any minute now the phone will be ringing. Can't go far from the phone, because she'll be ringing.

She told me.

One hour, two hours, three hours, anyway it didn't matter after that because I got pissed, and she never rang.

It was the festive season and the build up to Christmas 2004, a time to be merry. Was it compulsory?

Such an angelic smile and so sincere, it was so fair dinkum when she looked me in the eyes and reckoned – she'd ring me.

This was torture.

The first five times she said she was gunna ring me and she didn't, I just put it down to her being pretty busy.

The next five times she said she was gunna ring me and she didn't, I put it down to maybe unforseen circumstances, like a family crises, car accidents, food poisoning and stuff.

The next five times I started to feel something wasn't quite adding up, but maybe I was just overreacting?

The phone finally rang but it wasn't her, but all the same at least it rang, at least its working. It was a positive sign, things were on the up.

A friend had put a good word in for me with this nightclub mob in Darwin. They were planning this big Christmas party, and one of the highlights of it was gunna be this whopping great BBQ spectacular. My name had come up because everyone knows I can really handle myself on a BBQ. Next minute I've got the job. I'm the chef at this nightclub for their Christmas day festivities. The pay was pretty good, a couple of hundred bucks plus free drinks.

It's funny because when you're down in the dumps sometimes it only takes a little bit of good fortune to turn things around. It's like a domino effect, one thing leads to another, next minute you're on a roll.

So I rang up the girl that never rang, and she said she was busy can she ring me back?

Two days later the phone was still silent.

No point getting worked up, no point fearing the worst, I'm sure there'd be a perfectly rational explanation.

She was probably abducted by aliens.

Christmas day came around and I headed into the nightclub about mid morning ready for the cook up. I so desperately needed the two hundred dollars it wasn't funny, and the free drinks would no doubt help get me low self-esteem out of the gutter.

Once at the club they positioned the BBQ not real far from the dance floor and close enough to the big front bay windows for a little ventilation. So I was right in the action.

Quite a crowd fronted up for the big day and I really put me head down sizzling up a storm. Steaks snags and satays were flying left right and centre. The arvo rolled on and so did the free drinks.

Maybe in retrospect I did hit it a bit hard and sometime around sunset they kicked me out. I never even got a chance to hang up the tongs.

A week later after haggling they finally paid me the two hundred dollars.

That was a Minor Success.

Then I got pulled over that night by the police who were breath testing everyone. I hadn't been drinking so I was pretty pleased with myself when I announced to the Coppers that I don't touch the stuff.

Next minute a really young Cop comes out of the shadows and points excitedly to a small crack in the windscreen.

'Oh no' they all reckoned 'It's a cracked windscreen'!

Well, off they went, it was like they'd just heard the news, Haley's comet was gunna collide with the earth, and they were running around everywhere. They officially defected my old Toyota, which meant I couldn't drive it on the road again till I'd replaced the windscreen.

Christmas 2004 was going from bad to worse.

I needed a shoulder, a friend, a confidante, and a lover. I needed some company someone to spark me up a bit, so I rang the girl who never rang.

I'd caught her having dinner with her father, and she said she'd ring me straight back after they'd finished eating.

Something must have happened, maybe the old boy choked on a bone? Or, maybe a flock of migrating Siberian Wood-ducks ran into the power line outside her house during a dense fog, causing her phone to be down for a while.

Whatever the rational reason was, the girl that never rang... never rang.

Christmas 2004 had officially turned to shit.

The windscreen bloke reckoned it was my lucky day, they had one in stock and it was gunna only cost me two hundred dollars. One thing for sure, I didn't have to brush any cobwebs off the two hundred, it was moving way too quick.

Next step was the Vehicle Inspection centre to show them the new windscreen.

No need to worry about cleaning up or disguising all the oil leeks coming from underneath I figured, because all they just want to check is the new windscreen, and that should be it... no worries.

I don't know where I got that idea.

The inspector marched out of the shed like a Sergeant Major came to attention and signalled me to drive into the shed and go over the pit, as if to do a full all over rip roaring inspection. I hung me head out the window quite confused, 'If your just gunna check the windscreen why can't you just do it here'? I asked.

But this bloke wasn't mucking around, he sensed blood, he sensed a real kill coming up. His eyes rolled back in their sockets and his head swung wildly from side to side. The vehicle inspector had just turned into some type of monster right before my eyes. He was conjuring up some wild voodoo and he was gunna deliver the full wrath of the department down on me old humble Toyota.

Over the pit I drove and nervously applied the hand brake.

I could hear him under the car salivating.

Then another couple of his regimental mates got under there and it sounded like they were having sex. With each new oil leak they found it just heightened their frenzy, and their gurgling sounds got louder.

Once it was over I was handed volumes of repairs I had to

make to the vehicle to get it roadworthy again.

Christmas 2004 was getting very dismal, and although I didn't want to use bad language during the festive period, I found myself screaming the word 'Fuck' quite regularly on the way home.

They did me like a dinner, and now as if Christmas 2004 wasn't going bad enough the Toyota was grounded till I won 'X-lotto' or found a compassionate mechanic... and I didn't like me chances with either.

Well anyway there wasn't much else that could go wrong, I was off the road, no money, no prospects and in love with the girl that never rang.

What more could Christmas 2004 cough up?

That night I caught a bus into town and headed for the 'Pub Bar', a friendly little place on Mitchell Street.

It was really quiet as I dragged myself through the door, just a drunk Scottish bloke and a couple of nice looking women in their twenties. My timing was pretty good for a change, the two girls wanted to play some eight ball, so we decided to play doubles with me teaming up with the Scottish guy who proceeded to pass out on the eight ball table halfway through the game. The barman rang him a taxi, which left the two friendly girls and me.

This was great; this is what the festive season is all about I'm thinkin. There were two of them and one of me, and with any luck at least one of them might be as hard up as what I was.

The barman eventually called last drinks some time around midnight, so because we were all getting on so good we agreed to kick on to another bar called 'Squires Tavern' for a few more games of eight ball.

Along the boulevards of Darwin we strolled cracking jokes and stuff, and I was thinking to myself how much I like these spontaneous type nights where it all seems to happen.

Well, I thought it was happening, but in a few minutes it was really gunna seriously happen and I would have never predicted anything so huge, and also something so unexpected could ever happen to me over this bleak Christmas period.

We got to Squires, and one of the girls noticed this gentlemen's club next door called 'Sinsations'. 'Hey' She reckoned... 'let's go in!'

So the three of us detoured and went into Sinsations.

The blonder one of the two girls was tickled pink we'd stumbled across an establishment that specialised in the recreational activity of the removal of women's attire.

I'm thinkin' this nights getting more interesting by the minute.

In we went, the entry fee was ten dollars and the two girls shouted me, I think by the way I looked they knew I was a man that wasn't packin a real lot of cash. A sexy middle-aged lady at the door was pretty happy to get three late nighters wandering in, and she was all smiles.

The blonder of the two girls once again showed her enthusiasm and asked if she was allowed to get up and do a pole dance herself?

'Of course that will be fine', says the lady taking the money.

'I did a bit of dancing back in the Gold Coast' the blond girl reckoned.

I'm thinkin'...very interesting.

As soon as we went in and she saw the stage it was on for young and old. She sprung up there and grabbed the pole like it was a long lost friend and immediately started to get her gear off in time to the music.

I'm thinkin... eh!

Nakedly she squirmed and she twisted and she slid up and down the shiny chrome pole like a mangrove snail.

I'm thinkin'... farrrrrrrk!!

This girl really knew her stuff, and I'm sure the other dozen or so blokes that rushed to the edge of the stage would agree. Not only did she bend over backwards to show everyone her G spot, she also showed them H, I, J and K as well.

I felt like I was at a Gynaecology lecture at Uni.

For a while there I didn't know where to look, but then I figured staring was a pretty good option. Her friend was wildly cheering her on and some of the other blokes were throwing five and ten dollar notes. The air conditioning inside Sinsations was battling to keep up with the heat that she was generating, but of course it was all very tastefully done.

Eventually she puffed out a bit and slowly put her clothes back on and grabbed the money. Every one knew they had just witnessed something pretty special, maybe even historic. It reminded me of one of those great footballers that eventually retire after an illustrious career, but then comes back and plays that one last exhibition match, just for the crowd.

But she still had a bit more to give and in-between the regular performers she'd spring up and into it again. All up she probably stripped and re-stripped again about ten times.

Three o'clock came and there was only the three of us left, one girl cheering wildly, one girl naked sliding up and down the pole... and me. I started to work on a bit of mathematics.

I knew that Albert Einstein came up with a handy equation $E=MC^2$ and that revolutionised the laws of Physics.

So using that as my guide I came up with...

Exited Pole Dancer + Very Exited Friend x Me = Recreational Activities back at someone's place.

This equation was set to revolutionise Christmas 2004 and have a huge influence on the rest of my life. I was staring down the barrel of a huge and extremely raunchy Major Success. For once in my life I'd been in the right place at the right time.

Sinsations was coming to a close and I was starting to break out into a sweat wondering what action the rest of the night would bring. With the last of her buttons done up we headed out into the night, I was so exited, and the anticipation was unbearable. Then a car pulled up with two lads in it and the girls jumped in and they roared off.

Shit no.

It's not meant to end like this.

What the?

I'm thinkin', you wouldn't have to be a stunned mullet to work out I stood there like a stunned mullet.

The funny thing is I did see them make a mobile phone call in-between strips a while back but I never put two and two together because that wasn't the equation I was working on at the time.

As the car screeched around the corner she hung her head out and yelled 'Hope you enjoyed the show Phil', and then she disappeared in a cloud of burnt rubber.

Phil did enjoy the show, but another Major Success had mercilessly eluded me and to make things worse it was one of those rare Adults Only Major Successes - and they're hard to come by.

During the two-hour walk home I only thought it appropriate to wind things back a bit to just a basic Minor Success. Christmas 2004 had almost flared up into some wild festive interaction but a hot Commodore had just extinguished any hope of that.

Though tonight had been a great Christmas present, and it did unwrap itself, my heart once again sunk. It was back to reality, back to the status quo, back to a down and out dismal unproductive lonely Christmas 2004.

Into the tepid, damp early morning silence I wandered.

Hey... I wonder if anyone had been trying to ring me while I'd been out?

HE WAS JUST A QUIET CROC

The longest job I ever had, and probably one of the most interesting was when I worked as a Crocodile Farmer in north-east Arnhem Land. I was there from the end of 1991 to the beginning of 1994, and I must admit there weren't too many dull moments.

From going out and collecting croc eggs from the wild for incubation, to catching and trapping adult crocs for breeding, to many days hunting scrub cattle and buffalo, in an attempt to help feed all the hungry inmates. It was a real adventure and the thrills and spills and Minor Successes were numerous. The local Aboriginal people or 'Yolngu' as they are called opened their doors and made me feel welcome, and they taught me a lot about their amazing part of the country.

I made a lot of good mates, but as enjoyable as it was I suppose after a few pretty solid years I decided to move on. Australia is a big place and I wanted to have a bit more of a look around before I finally put the cue in the rack.

Everyone understood, and there were no worries.

But I wanted to leave the farm in the best order possible before I took off.

Everything was travelling pretty well, but there was a large croc named Gunyangara that had been living by himself in a pond that was really designed for growing out hatchlings. For two reasons this wasn't any good, firstly a croc like Gunyangara should be paired off with a female and utilized as far as breeding was concerned. Secondly, instead of having one big croc laying there doing bugger all, there should be about 100 juvenile crocs growing up in there turning themselves into some good money for the farm. But moving him had been one of those jobs I never got around to doing because there just never seemed the time, and probably because he was so big, the whole thing just got put on the backburner.

Gunyangara was an impressive croc, about four and a half metres and still growing. He was girthy as well, and I'm not sure what he would have weighed in at, but I don't reckon you would have got much change out of half a ton.

We all thought he had a quiet personality, relatively speaking of course. I mean a few other crocs on the farm were pretty toey, but the natures of crocodiles vary a bit from lizard to lizard and Gunyangara was very laid back... or so it seemed.

At least once a week, we'd go into his pen and clean all the green slime that builds up on the concrete. He'd lay there completely relaxed as we swept the concrete around him with these stiff bristled brooms and then hose it all down. We never had a problem; just his eyes would follow you around the pen as you worked and that was it.

He was just a quiet croc, a real gentleman, almost passive.

So just before I left the farm I organised to move him out of his pen and then hopefully put him in with a female and get him earning his keep.

The plan was for me to get in there and noose him, then with some help drag him into a cage then carry it across and release him in another pen.

Fairly straight forward, especially taking into account he was such a quiet croc.

About ten blokes had turned up to help with the carrying of the cage and I had the noose all ready to go. The noose consisted of a rope threaded through a three or four inch wide and two metre long length of PVC pipe. The rope had a lasoo type knot at one end, and the idea was to poke the croc a bit with the PVC and get him to open his jaws up. Then you just slip the noose over his top jaw, and about half way along is a large tooth, once you get over that pull the rope and tighten the noose behind that tooth, and you've got him. Then to calm him down a bit throw a wet towel across his eyes like a

blindfold, and then drag him into the cage and carry him over to his waiting bride. Then undo the rope and let him go, all very easy.

This was the basic concept anyway, and I'd like a dollar for every time someone said 'It shouldn't be a problem, because he's a quiet croc'.

There was no need to worry, no need to get nervous, no big deal at all, take a deep breath, time to get the job done... quiet croc.

Gunyangara was laying on the edge of his pond half in and half out of the water, looking very relaxed as usual, almost dopey, just his eyes followed my every move.

I slowly approached him.

Raising the PVC pole and the noose, I gave him a poke around the ribs to get him to open up his jaws so I could slip the noose over.

That was the last thing I remember with any real focus.

Gunyangara exploded out of the pond and lunged straight for me with horrifying speed. In the blink of an eye half a ton of croc was going to be all over me like a rash, then sucking on me like a 'Paddle Pop'.

Everyone reckoned he was a quiet croc, but obviously no-one had explained that to him. The news hadn't filtered through. He hadn't got the mail.

My ten helpers standing outside the pen couldn't believe Gunyangara's terrifying bloodthirsty rush, but they were even more surprised at the speed that I noosed him. 'Bloody hell did you see that'! I could hear them all excitedly saying.

I think I used up every bit of luck I was ever destined to have in one lifetime, right there in that pen - all in one go.

As the big croc came at me he somehow flew straight into the noose, and noosed himself! It was a million to one; the rope went perfectly over his top jaw behind the tooth and bang.

I had absolutely nothing to do with it. I just happened to be the bloke holding the pole. I never told the other blokes, they still think it was sheer speed and skill on my behalf.

The rest of the operation was a breeze and we carried the cage with the big bastard in it over to the other pen and let him go. It all went so well, everyone reckoned.

But I felt a lot more relaxed once I went home - had eight cans - and changed me underwear.

'THE BIG DAY OUT' ... AND A NIGHT OF 'INXS'

I MET PHOTOGRAPHER Sophie Howarth at an Aboriginal cultural festival in Arnhem Land. She was the talented chick up from Sydney and I was just the bloke cooking stew in the camp kitchen doing my bit to keep everyone going for the week long bush festival.

Everyday she'd front up for a feed, bowl in hand, and a chirpy grin. Sophie had something about her, maybe you could call it good looks, or maybe it was just her energy for life, but she had a real attraction.

What ever it was, she was giving off more radiation than the x-ray machine at Royal Darwin hospital.

I wouldn't say I did me nuts straight off, but I was definitely heading in that general direction.

But Sophie already had a love in her life, and that was photography.

She lived for it.

There was no time to be burdened with a loser from the bush hanging around. All the same we did become friends over the course of the festival. Then after it was over I didn't really think I'd ever see her again. Later that year I went down to Adelaide to visit family and guess who I run into at the airport?

Sophie.

She was as nice as ever with about 22 cameras wrapped around her in various stages of readiness. Some were slung over her shoulders, some hanging out of her pockets and a bunch around her neck. She was towing a suitcase behind her that was no doubt full of film to feed her growing family of cameras.

Sophie lit up the domestic terminal like a flash of lightning and the crowd got out the way as her and her swarm of cameras swung on through.

'Phil... how are they hanging'? She screeched.

'Fairly low', I replied, in all sincerity.

She took my photo a few times and we caught up on each other's news. Sophie was in town for the 'Big Day Out' concert, as the official photographer. 'Got to get some killer shots', she howled excitedly, like a dingo giving birth. 'Nothing's bigger than the Big Day Out!'

'Phil its gunna be huge! Get your arse down there!' Sophie demanded, in full soprano. With a flick of the wrist she placed a ticket in my hand, smiled, bolted for a taxi and was gone. All of a sudden the domestic terminal went dim again as I stood there examining the ticket.

Big Day Out – Admit one.

Interesting...

Two hot Adelaide days later I'm walking into the Big Day Out concert at the old Wayville showgrounds. Not a worry in the world, a couple of coldies will do me, and a little light entertainment, what a great way to relax in good old sunny Adelaide, I'm thinkin.

My last really big concert was 'Slim Dusty' live in Darwin,

Sophie Howarth

and whichever way you looked at it, old Slim was going to be a bloody hard act to follow.

But I could tell right from the start this was no ordinary show. I went through the gate with a herd of wild looking young people, and I really felt my age; I must have looked like someone that had arrived to pick up their kids. It wasn't long and I was confronted with a wall of sound that parted me hair fair down the middle and pinned me ears back. It was like a jet taking off and I was standing behind the motor.

I'd played a bit of rock and roll in my younger days, but this band was playing that loud some of my fillings were starting to shake loose.

More excited wild young people pushed me along, and we were stampeding in the direction of the noise. It was a reckless frenzy and definitely no time to lose your footing unless you wanted to be trampled to death.

My inner organs vibrated to the beat, as I feared for my life.

Through the soundwaves and the sweat I could see the band responsible. It was all pretty desperate; every few minutes the singer would jump off the stage into the crowd, probably trying to get away from the band and escape the shit music, but the crowd with their arms outstretched would catch him and roll him back onto the stage.

Poor bastard.

He wanted out but there was no way out, and he was stuck with the loudest band that had ever plugged in. I'm wondering if suburbs around Adelaide were getting any electricity, or was this mob using it all up? I'd say at a rough guess there were probably some blackouts.

I'll never forget it.

Now, at this stage I thought this was it; this was the 'Big Day Out'.

I had no idea other stuff was happening.

Then a girl next to me reckoned to her friend, 'Let's go see another band'. Of-course I didn't hear her say it, I was lip-reading because of the noise.

Well I'll be buggered, there's more! Bloody hell.

So I took off, managing to break through the sound barrier and get far enough away to hear myself think a bit.

After walking for a while and sidestepping crazed wild young people goin the other way, I came across this chilled out area they called the 'Lily Pad'.

The Lily Pad was in complete contrast to what I had just come from. There was a DJ playing some laid back 70's music at about one quarter of the decibels that the previous band was cranking out. There was an air of calm among the wild young people. Everyone was slumped on beanbags and old couches and they looked like someone had shot them all with a tranquilliser dart.

I don't know what they were on, but you can bet it wasn't 'Victoria Bitter'.

Some of this mob was up there with the Space Shuttle.

I half thought about curling up on a bean bag for a minute and give me eardrums a rest when I noticed a huge line up of people a little further up the track... might be something exciting goin on.

On closer inspection it was no big deal, just wild young people lining up for the toilet, and by the looks of the ones staggering out it must have been hell inside.

I think some of them were in a state of shock, but the Saint John Ambulance was close at hand to help anyone that went down.

Time to poke up wind a bit, so I followed the general stream of people heading along the road to somewhere. I had no idea what was around the corner but it must be pretty serious judging by the look on their faces.

I felt like an explorer in a new land.

We all ended up at this very dark bunker type structure aptly named 'The Boiler-Room', it was like an underground car park occupied by a crowd of young people with glazed over looks in their eyes. Everyone was sucking on bottled water milling around hypnotized by the constant doof doof doof music blaring out of strategically placed speakers. Intermittently people would bounce around limply to the doof doof drumbeat. I think they were all getting ready to start mating.

It was serious business.

I hung around for about twenty minutes waiting for the singing to start but it never did. Just this relentless drumbeat and wild young people jumping around like brolgas out on the flat.

Maybe I should have started up a conversation with someone and got into it a bit but what's a bloke talk about in a place like this - the drum?

All the same, it was something completely different and I was finding the Big Day Out concert pretty interesting.

I couldn't help but wonder how the demure Sophie fitted in to all this, but when you look at it, photography is all about capturing the moment, and there was plenty of them.

The drumbeat started to really pump up a bit causing the crowd to go into a concerted stagger. Obviously this was one of their favourites.

The Boiler-room was starting to really cook, but I'd absorbed about as much drum as God had intended a bloke to hear in one lifetime, so I weaved me way through the crowd getting splashed by bottled water, trying not to get bowled over, and trying to keep an eye out for Sophie.

The entrance that I came in was totally blocked by possessed wild young people so there was no way I could get out, I was trapped.

I'm thinkin' if this mob works out I'm twenty years older

than they are they're likely to tear me limb from limb. I could see the headlines in the local Adelaide Advertiser 'Old bloke dies in the Boiler room'.

It was time to make like a tree, and get rooted.

I saw some daylight filtering through on the other side of the Boiler room and I figured it was my only chance, I loped across the dance floor like a wounded Bush Turkey, so as not to attract any attention, and then it was up some steps and out of there.

A gentle breeze washed over me helping to dry off the beads of perspiration that had formed on my forehead during the Boiler-Room breakout. If I had to write down the ten 'must do' things before I die, I don't think hangin out at the Boiler room will make the list, I'm definitely thinkin.

Long awaited freedom and the fresh air inspired me and so I joined in with a little mob of wild young people galloping along a pathway and up some more steps, and then all of a sudden I could see what the Big Day Out was all about. No wonder why Sophie was raving on about it so much.

I was over looking what was once an oval, jam packed with thousands of heaving wild Aussie youth, treading water in an ocean of pure adrenalin.

This was the main event and there was no looking back.

I've done a lot of dangerous things in my day, catching crocs and stuff like that, but there was no way I was going near that crowd, I mean a bloke's got to draw the line somewhere.

Lights flashed across the stage and the band whopped it right into them. It was an awe-inspiring sight, not quite sunset at Uluru but in its own way just as spectacular. The music was loud and aggressive but it wasn't half bad, and I started to enjoy it a bit.

My thoughts once again moved onto Sophie, being the

official photographer I'd reckon she'd be up near the stage or even on it, snapping away. I don't know what the mortality rate of photographers is at the Big Day Out but I'd say they would lose a few. She sure had guts mixing it up with this mob.

The music roared on into the beautiful Adelaide dusk, rocking the multitude.

After experiencing the Big Day Out in all its decibelled glory, I had an even stronger respect for Sophie Howarth and her photographic love affair. This was no nine to five office job she was holding down, this was the Big bloody Day Out, and I hoped like hell she somehow survived it.

As I come away from there and headed up town for a well-deserved beer and an uncrowded toilet, I really didn't think I'd ever see or experience anything like that again. But that's life for you, just when you think you've seen it all there's always something else around the corner to broaden a bloke's horizons a little bit more, and even as I'm writing this, I can't believe the situations I get myself into.

The very next year I returned again from the Northern Territory for a bit of a holiday and once again catch up with family. During the course of that year I'd met a really interesting bloke by the name of Andrew Farris. A very talented musician and songwriter, Andrew was a member of one of the all time great rock bands 'INXS'. He'd been up in Arnhem Land doing some music workshops with the Aboriginal kids from that area. A very likable person Andrew fitted in very well with his easygoing style, and he had no airs or graces usually associated with a person of his acclaim.

In other words, he wasn't up himself.

So it was New Year's Eve and I was in Adelaide wondering

how I was gunna see it in. It was just by pure chance I rang up a mate in the Territory just to wish him all the best, he'd also been working on these music workshops as well, and he gave me the good oil on the INXS concert later that night. Catch up with Andrew Farris he reckoned, and he gave me Andrew's mobile number. So I rang him, not really thinking too much about it, I knew INXS were a huge band and all that, but living mostly in the bush I suppose I just never realised the magnitude of their popularity. I'd just spent the last twelve months sitting around the campfire listening to Slim Dusty cassettes so I wasn't mentally prepared. I just saw me and Andrew having a beer and a yarn on New Year's Eve, which was about the size of it - low key.

'G'day mate how you goin?' Andrew reckoned.

He was pretty pumped up getting ready for the show but he spared a few minutes for a chat then told me to meet him in the foyer of the Hilton Hotel in half an hour, and he'd give me a free pass to the concert.

You ripper! I'm thinkin, at last me New Year's Eve is taking on some direction. I strode into the Hilton dead on time for the rendezvous with Andrew, and what a place.

I'm thinkin, if I sold everything I own, which is an old Toyota, a swag and a guitar, I'd probably be able to afford to stay there a few nights.

I was in the middle of a daydream when Andrew rocked up; he was looking really sharp and chaffing at the bit to get on stage. I tried to talk him into having a beer but he didn't have the time, then he pulled out this envelope from his jacket, and a serious look swept across his face.

He looked me fair in the eye, then he looked down at the envelope, then back at me.

I'm thinking shit, what's he got in there, the 'Holy Grail'?

As he pulled out its contents the Hilton Hotel foyer seemed to go quiet, it was an eerie silence as Andrew slowly revealed a small piece of plastic, and inscribed on it was the words 'INXS Access all Areas'.

I could swear I heard people gasp when it came into view. What's goin on?

It just looked like a normal bit of plastic with writing on it.

After draping the sacred plastic symbol around my neck Andrew took off.

Well I'll be buggered, what a great bloke I'm thinking, as I naively headed off down the road with this thing around me neck. I suppose it took me about forty minutes to find me way in the foot falcon to the place on the edge of town where the concert was.

It was a real nice balmy evening and plenty of activity around the streets of Adelaide. The show was outdoors and was the culmination of a big car race they have annually.

Excited people were everywhere as I got close to one of the entry areas.

Now, I'm one of those blokes that have never really got anything for nothing, so it felt strange approaching the gate thinking I was gunna just stroll through, and not pay anything, because of this plastic tag around my neck. At any moment I expected some security bloke to come out of nowhere grab me, and get me in a headlock for trying to sneak in without paying. But the crowd parted as I came through, and the security blokes ushered me in with smiles and it was all very dignified, and also very unbelievable.

It was like I was Prince Charles and Moses at the Red Sea, all rolled into one.

Well cut me right ball off and call me lefty I'm thinkin, as I headed for the INXS concert with the sacred chunk of plastic dangling from me neck.

The crowd was a mixed bag, some wild looking young ones but also a lot of groovy older types. Probably because the band had been around for several years, and they were that good, their music appealed to all sorts of people.

INXS had just come on, and Port Augusta Power Station had nothing on the electricity this band was generating. Lights, hysteria, wailing guitar and 10,000 people going mad. Well, 9,999 were going mad actually, I was stuck right at the back, and the bloke in front of me had his missus perched up on his shoulders, which apart from me not being able to see, wasn't a real problem.

The problem was her bum crack.

It was at head height and about six inches in front of my nose, and because we were all jammed up like sardines I couldn't get around it. I knew if I kept getting pushed from behind me face is gunna be right up against it. Then my worst fears were realised, I did get shoved from behind and me face was fair flush up against it, and it wasn't pretty.

I rode it out for a few songs staring deeper and deeper into this woman's arse crack. The music was great but I came to the conclusion this was no way to enjoy the show, so I slid out of there and headed off looking for the bar. INXS were very good but I suppose I've never been one for the big crowds.

Next to the concert was a huge flood lit car park and it looked like there might just be a bar set up on the other side so I cut through.

Next minute out of nowhere, I see this huge security guy running straight towards me.

Typical, now I'm gunna get kicked out because he probably thinks I'm pinching stuff out of the cars.

'Hey Mate' he yelled, and he only had eyes for one thing, and that was the plastic INXS Access all Areas tag around me neck.

I never realized the actual power this humble bit of plastic possessed. Naturally I went straight on the defensive explaining how hard it was to see at the back of the crowd and stuff, and he just took another look at the plastic tag and said excitedly, 'Follow me!' - and then he ran off.

So there we are running through the car park, and I had no idea what the hell was going on, and where we were running to? I was battling to keep up, but we weaved our way out of the car park, across the flat, and around some marquee and headed for some stairs.

Up the stairs we ran and through some curtain type thing hanging down, and I'm on the stage, I'm on the stage with INXS!

The security guy gave me the thumbs up and took off. I was so close to the drummer every time he swung his head around doin a drum roll his sweat was splashing onto me. I couldn't believe it, I'd gone from the arse crack at the back, to the stage!

Talk about a Major Success.

Andrew Farris was there jumping from keyboards to guitar giving it everything he had, he was so close I felt like slappin him on the back.

On they rocked, INXS tearing shreds off the 9,999 screaming fans with Phil O'Brien standing there next to the drummer completely untouchable with me plastic tag of holiness strapped to me neck. I could have just grabbed a guitar and started playing along, and they still probably wouldn't have kicked me out.

Besides Nuclear Power, the INXS Access all Areas tag was

probably one of the most powerful things on earth, and I just couldn't believe I was the one wearing it.

The concert finally came to an end and through all the screaming and lights and commotion the band filed past me heading for the stairs. Andrew Farris came past and reckoned 'See you backstage at the after party Phil'.

He didn't seem surprised to see me on the stage either, it was like - that's where you always end up when you've got the sacred plastic tag, it just leads you there by its wonderful powers. Andrew obviously knew that when he gave it to me.

So now, not only have I miraculously ended up on stage with INXS but I've just been invited to the backstage after party. My head really started to spin... I had decisions to make.

Now being at an INXS backstage after party I'd probably have to have sex with roughly somewhere between 8-14 hot groupie chicks. That just went without saying. Also there's gunna be heaps of heavy drugs like cocaine, I mean, that's pretty standard with these world famous rock bands. What am I gunna do I'm thinkin?

I'd never tried heavy drugs but if I'm gunna have so much sex I'm probably, realistically speaking, gunna need something to keep me goin, enhance me performance.

Anyway that was my reasoning at the time.

So with the decision making process out the way I headed down the steps ready to give it my all at the INXS after party.

It's gunna be totally unbelievable.

We'll probably rage for days.

The adrenaline started to really pump like mad, then as I entered the marquee the adrenaline stopped pumping.

There was the band sitting down relaxing with their wives

and families, and they were drinking 'Low Alcohol Beer'.

INXS must have matured, mellowed out, and got family orientated, and that's great, good on em, but why the fuck did they pick this week?

It was about then I figured I might reclassify the Major Success to a Minor Success.

The low alcohol beer was the clincher.

I looked down at me 'INXS Access all Areas' plastic tag and nervously stroked it, but the magic was gone, I'd accessed all the areas, and there was nowhere left to access.

But a bloke shouldn't be too disappointed, as it turned out I finally did get to have a beer and a yarn with Andrew Farris, one of natures true gentlemen, and it was a New Years Eve I'll never forget.

Bum crack at the back - to centre stage.

If it didn't happen to me, I wouldn't have believed it.

The sacred plastic symbol!

MY FINEST HOUR

AND SO IT CAME TO PASS ...
   I'd finally made it to the top. The pinnacle.
   I was part of the big one. I'd ascended into glory.
   I was at the top of my game.
   I'd peaked out.
   The ultimate act of distinction.
   No, I didn't become an astronaut and land on the moon.
   No, I didn't light the Olympic flame, and
   No I hadn't woken up next to Elle MacPherson.
   It was way bigger than any of those things.

People present were moved greatly as I sucked down the historic brew.
   'Look at him go' they all whispered, as the camera rolled and I swung the cold green tin up to my lips.
   'Don't forget Phil three gulps with the Adams Apple, two's too woosy and four's being a pig'! The director yelled - trying to get the best out of his leading man.
   Me.
   I'd finally scored an acting role I could get my teeth into and for an amateur actor like me, and a huge Victoria Bitter drinker, it just doesn't get any bigger. It was a national VB ad

and my job was to wop one down.

'Nice work Phil' the director blasted, 'but can we just get it one more time'?

'Phil, just scoop the can up, don't jerk it, and be natural'!

Shit no I'm thinkin, not another can.

We were on take fifteen and I was really starting to feel the effects.

'Cut! Cut! – Phil, too much tongue more lip, more lip, suck that can, c'mon mate suck that can'.

'O.K. action'!

Oh fuck, another one, they must think I'm a fish.

'Cut! Cut'!

'Phil we saw the bar-code on the can, we don't want to see the bar-code on the can, cover it with your fingers'.

'Action, go, Phil reach in the esky, out of the ice, lovely, lovely, oh yeah, go mate, suck it'.

'Nice work Phil, cut'.

'Probably a bit slow getting out of the esky Phil can we go again please'?

I'm thinkin', does this mob think I've got hollow legs or something, where do they think I'm putting all the grog? I mean I like me Victoria Bitter but hey, I'm only flesh and blood.

'Action'!

Gulp, gulp, gulp, and gulp.

'Cut, sorry mate that was four gulps with the Adams Apple, it's gotta be three, just back off a bit'.

I'll back off all right, I'll pass out.

Take 25 – I could feel me legs going.
Take 28 – Me Bladders telling me it can't hold it much longer.
Take 29 – Me stomach reckons, 'me too'.

Take 30 – Eyes starting to hang out of their sockets.

Take 30 something, the director yells 'It's a wrap, thankyou everyone'.

I staggered over to the nearest tree and had a leak that went for eight minutes. My body had been pushed to the limit, just like an elite athlete, I'd gone through the pain barrier.

'Someone call a Taxi'! Screamed the director... 'Phil's rotten'.

Skulling a can of VB in a national beer commercial for a big VB drinker like me was probably on par with winning Gold at the Olympics. You'd risen to the top of the field through hard work and dedication and there you are in the spotlight with all the accolades showering down on you. Moments don't come any sweeter.

The journey to get there had been a long gruelling and also a very competitive one.

About four weeks prior I'd heard about this big VB television ad they were making and they were filming bits of it all over Australia. It was gunna be a real hum dinger. One section of it was to be filmed in Darwin, so when auditions were called I thought bugger it, I'll have a go at that.

I knew I had style and endurance when it comes to sinking coldies and I felt quietly confident. I had experience on my side as well, and there's nothing like an old dog for a gravel road I always say.

So I headed down to Burundi Studios in Darwin where the auditions were taking place. There were blokes lined up for miles, the word was out and the big VB drinkers had gathered from everywhere. I recognised blokes from towns hundreds of miles away. Everyone was trying their luck; outback looking types, brick laying continental looking types, uni students, army guys, doctors, lawyers and even a few office workers dressed up in singlets and shorts trying to look tough.

It was a big field, and I had me work cut out.

I was going to have to out think this mob.

Somehow I had to get the edge.

So seeing there was about half an inch of bulldust sitting on the dash of my Toyota after the last bush trip, I decided to use it as make up. Running my hand through it I coated my face and arms and put a bit in my hair. All of a sudden I had that swarthy ruddy complexion giving me that 'this bloke really needs a beer look'. It was a masterstroke.

I took my place in line with all the others and finally my number came up, and so I threw myself into the audition with everything I had.

I'd never reached into an esky and cracked a can with so much precision so much feeling. It was a priceless performance. Like a ballet dancer I had all the attributes they were looking for... flexibility, grace and poise, and I think the ruddy complexion really sealed it.

A fortnight later someone from Melbourne rings up.

'Congratulations! Outstanding work at the audition, would you like to be in the new national classic Victoria Bitter ad?'

'My oath' I reckoned, with patriotic pride.

Then, I immediately went into training.

I cracked a few at home, and then I went for a light walk on the beach and cracked a couple. I cracked cans at sunset, sunrise, and I even faced Mecca and cracked one. Over the next weeks in between me can cracking regime I also worked on me esky technique as well, trying to get a nice sweeping motion in and out of the ice. Developing a good knee bend was important, and also the hip swivel when exiting the esky with the can was important.

Representing the VB drinkers of Australia was serious business.

I wanted to be in peak condition mentally as well as physically so I hired the 'Rocky' video, it really helped to get me in the zone, and the fundamentals of the Rocky movie were very similar to the ones I employed during my intense training. Where as Rocky shadow boxed his way through the streets, and ran mile after mile then up 100's of rows of stairs to the top of a spectacular monument, and then shadow boxed some more. I walked down to the beach looked around a bit and then cracked one... with 'exactly' the same grit and determination.

There was no doubt about it, I was in about as good a form as a VB drinker can get.

I was ready.

The film crew turned up roughly about four weeks after the audition and they seemed like a pretty switched on mob of professionals. They were hand picked from all parts of Australia, the cream of the crop.

Obviously VB was planning to make a ball tearer and they weren't holding any horses back on this one.

Our day started with the sun and we all met as planned on the landing at Cullen Bay near Darwin. There was a flash cabin cruiser waiting to take us out to film the first part of the ad. I sort of had a rough idea what was going on but I wasn't really listening when the director was explaining the ins and outs. There was way more to this ad than just crackin a can, that's for sure.

Apparently I had to pull in a Barramundi and really look like I'm working up a thirst doing it. With the heat and humidity in Darwin that shouldn't be hard.

As we cruised along heading for the mangroves on the other side of the harbour a panic went through the film crew. The director reckoned my beard was a bit longer than when I went for the audition. All of a sudden he reckoned it wasn't the right look, and he was fair dinkum.

They had a big meeting, next minute the cry went out for scissors and someone's produced this big pair of scissors. Next minute the make up lady has got me pinned to this chair, she's on me lap and she's got her legs wrapped around me in an Indian leg lock. The director's behind her and he's giving instructions and the make up lady is coming at me with these huge scissors. She started throwing them around as if she was all set to perform the Macassan Sword dance!

It was whisker by whisker and I'm thinkin if the boat hits a bit of swell she's gunna take half me face off.

After a nervous fifteen minutes they had another meeting with me still pinned to the chair and they all reckoned that was - 'the look'.

The make up lady released me from the leg lock, and I got ready to do me bit.

The boat anchored and re-anchored about twenty times till the director was happy with the spot. Then they put me in a dinghy with these other two blokes and we floated back about ten metres from the cabin cruiser. I had a fishing rod and the line was tied to the bottom of the cabin cruiser, so it looked like I was doing battle with a good size fish.

'Work it Phil! 'Work it'! The director's yelling, and the other two blokes job was to pat me on the back while I'm jerking on the rod.

Every few goes they'd pull the dinghy back alongside the

cabin cruiser where the camera crew were and the make up lady would spray glycerine on me face to make it look like I had these big drops of sweat coming out of me. The sweat was pissing out of me anyway but she kept doing it. Well, we did that for about one hundred times till the director was happy and I'm thinkin, when do I get to crack the can?

I was tonguing for a coldie, but we had a long way to go yet.

This mob weren't just slappin one together; every second of this ad had been thought out and then re-thought out.

It had to be perfect.

'O.K. Phil, this is the money shot mate', the director's yellin.

They untied my line from the bottom of the cabin cruiser and threaded a hook onto it. Then they produced a good size Barramundi from a holding tank on the boat. They put the hook through the Barra and dropped it in the water. My job was to reel it in.

'Action'!

'C'mon Phil give mate give'.

When the Barra hit the water it looked around spat the hook out and roared off heading for East Timor.

'Cut, Cut'! - Bawled the director.

'Barry get another Barramundi out of the holding tank please', asked the director.

'O.K. Action'!

They dropped the second Barra in and it died straight away, it went belly up, it must have had a heart attack or something, it was stone dead.

'Bloody hell Barry', 'Cuuuuuuttt'!

'What is it with these fish'?

The next one luckily, danced perfectly across the top of the water as I reeled it in and they got some great shots. I was relieved a bit because by now it was heading towards midday

and getting pretty warm in that dinghy, and all the glycerine they were spraying on me wasn't helping either. It was like basting a pig on a spit, I was getting cooked.

'More glycerine'! Yelled the director; 'I want to really see those droplets', as the camera did a few close ups.

They were frying me like a tomato and it was jubilation when the director finally said he was happy, and it was a wrap.

Mid afternoon we made it back to the landing at Cullen Bay, I was feeling a bit rugged, I hadn't eaten much and was also a bit dehydrated with eyes stinging a bit from the glycerine. Of the other two blokes that were in the dinghy one wasn't too bad but the other was like a beetroot and his changing colour caused the director some concern because of the continuity issue.

The next scene and this is the one I'd been training for.

The big 'reach in the esky and suck the can'.

We went along to Fanny Bay a short drive down the foreshore and the camera crew set up for the big scene. They were using real beer and it was cold and it didn't touch the sides as I launched into the scene...take after take.

They wanted it perfect - it had to be perfect.

'Cut!'

'Go again Phil, c'mon mate, c'mon make love to that can'.

'Give it up mate c'mon', went the director.

Not bad let's go again, and again, and again.

I might have been well practiced and highly skilled but I was struggling.

That's when the training takes over.

You dig deep and you guts it right out.

Just like an Olympic marathon runner, they can never remember the last four or five miles of the race, they're just running on adrenalin.

Their minds shuts down, its do or die.

Well, that's exactly how it was with the last dozen cans. I can't really remember how I pulled it off.

After a leak that could have filled up two Jerry cans I'm getting put in a taxi, I had a pocket full of money, a complimentary carton of VB, a VB key ring a VB cap and a VB t-shirt.

It was a Minor Success that it was just a thirty second commercial, and not a full length movie otherwise I don't think I would have made it out alive.

What a day. I couldn't face another VB for about two months.

I'd come to represent the Victoria Bitter drinkers of Australia, and everyone knows they're an elite group.

It was an unforgettable patriotic feeling that flowed through my veins that day - alongside all the beer.

And was it my finest hour?

Pretty bloody close.

OLD TIMERS

WHAT SEEMS LIKE a life time ago I had a job with mining giants BHP. I was in a small mineral exploration crew working in the farming country around Central Victoria. BHP knew there were these deposits of what they call 'Mineral Sands' in that area. They needed to know if it was a viable deposit.

So basically, we're standing around in the sun on the side of the road drilling as many holes as we could to see what was down there.

I personally couldn't have given a stuff.

I personally couldn't have cared if we discovered 'Lasseter's Lost Reef'.

I just needed a few bucks, and I wanted to have a look at Victoria, because it was a place I'd never had much to do with.

So far I really liked the people I'd met around where we'd been working, they were good country stock, friendly, and seemed a hard working mob. A lot of the farms had been in the family for many years, and they had very proud histories.

One day we were drilling away next to this paddock and this really old tractor goes sailing past, and driving it was this elderly bloke who had to be at least eighty years of age.

The tractor looked like it was eighty years of age as well, it had an open cab and the old bloke bounced along and I'm thinkin 'Wow' the old fella's still hanging in there!

Ten minutes later this vintage car turns up. It was like one of those cars that gangsters used to drive around in back in the nineteen thirties. Out steps this bloke and he's face is wrinkled up and leathery like an Egyptian Mummy, and he's stooped over like a half sucked scorpion, and he must have been at least one hundred years old.

He slowly shuffled over and I said 'Gidday mate what are you up to'?

He nodded in the direction of the ancient tractor over in the paddock and reckoned...

'Just come down to see how me boy's workin'.

ONE VERY EMBARRASSING NIGHT

SEPTEMBER 2002 and the Northern Territory fashion awards were coming up, and although not renowned world-wide for it's 'Fashion Industry', the N.T was still home to a lot of creative clothes' designers, and this was their night. Anyone who could use a needle and thread and had a bit of imagination stepped up and put their best dress forward.

Stunning outfits came out of the woodwork and it was all culminating in the 'Award Night extravaganza'. The judges had made their decisions and the Top End fashion capital of Darwin was playing host to the gala awards. For that special one day of the year, Darwin was going to be a hotbed of style.

O.K, it wasn't quite Paris in springtime, but a lot of people put a lot of effort into their passion for fashion in the Territory. Out of a population of 200,000 people, 199,750 preferred to wear thongs, shorts, and a singlet, but that still left 250 people that had great fashion sense, and every one of them bought a ticket for the big night. So when you look at the numbers, that's 100% support.

'Yvette' ran her hand through her pretty 'thirty something' shaggy blonde hair, and felt as though she'd never pull this thing together in time. Charged with the responsibility of organising the big award night and the entertainment that went with it, she was at her wit's end. She had a great team of models lined up to strut the winning outfits, there were no worries there, and she had the Lord Mayor lined up to be the presenter, so no worries there, but she wanted it to be more than just your average 'Catwalk' turnout.

Yvette wanted to give the night a bit more of a twist, some Territory style humour, put on a real show. She knew she had some stunning looking female models but she wanted someone that could represent the majority of Territorians, the ones that were still wearing shorts and singlets and didn't give a stuff about style. An ambassador from the no taste part of society.

To her way of thinking it would be a type of fashion statement, get some down and out looking bloke with a pot guts and no fashion sense at all, throw him into the show, and take the piss out of him!

This is what they call art, and the half cut fashion fraternity of the N.T. were bound to really appreciate it. Time was running out, if such a bloke existed, she had to find him quick.

It had been a long day and Yvette needed a little time out for a few hours. Thursday night in Darwin meant Mindil Beach markets, it was a great place to unwind, grab a wine or a nice feed from one of the stalls and chill out and enjoy a stunning sunset.

Mindil Beach markets was one of Yvette's special places.

If only she could find her man, the missing link to her plans, a pot gutted fashion loser. If only...

Half way through strumming 'Me and Bobbi McGee' I knew it wasn't gunna work; it was just too bloody dark. It was the first time I'd ever had a gig at Mindil Beach playing me guitar to the sunset crowd, but I wish the organisers had supplied a bit of bloody lighting. I'd only started playing about fifteen minutes ago, but then the sun went down and I couldn't see me fingers and where to put em, and here I am announcing the show's over. Sorry everyone, can't see me fingers.

Actually, apart from that thirty something good looking lady with the blond hair that had been staring at me the whole time, I don't think anyone really cared.

How embarrassing, I'm dressed to the nines I've got me best thongs on, I've got me going out pair of shorts on and I've got me 'Sunday best' singlet on... no work gear, no way. I'd put a bit of effort into this gig, and now mose well pack up and go home.

I felt like a bit of a loser actually.

'Excuse me', 'Excuse me', came the voice through the post sunset darkness. 'My name's Yvette, and I thought you were great'!

Realizing my luck with women is bound to change one of these years, I'm constantly vigilante, but when I shook her hand her wedding finger had more rocks on it than Argyle Diamond mine, so I assumed she had other things on her mind besides recreation.

And she did.

'Would you be interested in being part of the Northern Territory Fashion awards?' she asked, and then she said I'd be absolutely perfect.

What could I say? This woman obviously knew talent when she saw it.

'I'd be honoured' I said.

She never really got around to telling me what I had to actually do, but rehearsals were on next night in town. 'Just be there' she said, and off she went happy as Larry.

It just goes to show you; one minute you're getting ready to eat a shit sandwich because the gig flopped, next minute you're Phil O'Brien on the Catwalk. Like I always said... you just can't keep a good man down.

Next night I rocked up to the rehearsal a little early, I was keen but this was a completely new thing for me, I'd never been part of the fashion world before and I was wondering how I would go. Would I fit in?

I doubted it very much, but Yvette seemed to think I had potential.

I parked up me old Toyota and wandered over.

Yvette hadn't opened up yet so the models had congregated out the front, and when I saw how good looking they all were me top lip curled straight back...and all of a sudden I realised how interested I'd always been in fashion.

What a great industry, I'm thinkin.

Apart from the fact I was 20 years older, twenty times fatter, twenty times uglier and about twenty times less likely to have anything to do with any of the girls socially, we all had a lot in common – we were there. These girls were hot, and I changed my mind from planning to ask Yvette how much money I'd get for being in the show, to how much I owed her for letting me be in the show.

The door opened and there was Yvette ushering everyone in and wasting no time in getting the models organised. She was very professional and quite charming the way she got things going.

It was another world; girls going through the motions of

their catwalk routines, others working on their turns, others stretching, and a few over in the corner trying on some outfits, but I tried not to perve too much and attract attention.

I just kept out the way and then Yvette came over and gave me a pep talk and filled me in on my particular role in the show.

It sounded like I had quite an unusual part to play, and my first reaction was a bit apprehensive. It was gunna be a very thin line between Yvette pulling off a good show, or me looking like a complete dickhead.

Or maybe me looking like a dickhead was all part of it.

Yvette knew what she was doing she said, this was no slap dash affair, people were paying top dollar to be there and her show was going to work, it was going to be a real expression of fashion in the Territory with a real Territory flavour, and it sounded so creative and artistic when she explained it.

I still didn't feel real sure about the whole thing, but then I looked around at the raging hot arse young models swaggering around, and I'm thinkin... Geez, I can't let the team down. So I told Yvette I'd give it me best shot.

The award night came around and as per instructions we all met backstage at the very swish Harry Chan function centre, and got ready for the show.

I took a peek through the curtain and checked out the crowd, and there were Ball gowns swaying, T.V cameras panning, Tuxedoes tuxing, Politicians chatting and Navy Admirals admiring each other's uniforms, it didn't look like Darwin out there, it was more like Monte Carlo or Milan. Waitresses appeared to be floating on air moving briskly around the room topping up champagne and zooming off again through the crowded Ball Room. There was genuine

Yvette (left) with one of her many 'very tidy' associates: Irina.

excitement amongst the 'Who's Who' and the 'Slaves of fashion', and the atmosphere was electric.

Backstage, all around me were beautiful girls in various stages of undress and I'm thinkin, this sure beats strumming 'Me and Bobbi McGee' in the dark at the Mindil Beach markets. Boobs were bouncing in and out, G- strings were being finely tuned, hair, make up, it was a frenzy... and I was frothing at the mouth. Now I know where Global Warming started. There was enough hot flesh getting around in there to melt the Polar Ice Caps.

Yvette rallied her troops; as it got close to start time, encouraging reassuring and helping with the outfits. I'd slipped into me gear for my first skit – footy shorts, thongs and a singlet.

Not quite the 'Gucci' outfit I was hoping for.

The Lord Mayor kicked the show off.

I sure hoped Yvette knew what she was doing.

She gave me the nod, and I had to chase a young model with a towel wrapped around her, across the stage behind the Lord Mayor.

Out we shot while he was doing the opening speech, the stunner in the towel with me in hot pursuit. It was meant to be just a bit of slapstick, something to break up the formality that usually accompanies these types of events.

No-one laughed, I think the crowd thought some bloke had got loose backstage and had lost control.

Where's the security? They're all thinkin.

No time to worry, a quick change into my jeans and shirt and get ready for 'Territory Leisure Wear'. An intro by the Lord Mayor and the girls slowly made their way onto the stage in time to some music and all mingled in as if at a typical Territory setting somewhere. It was a nice touch by Yvette, instead of the usual regimented up and down the catwalk one at a time, she had thought of other ways to showcase the fashion in a more day to day scenario, and I really felt she'd come up with a clever concept.

The Girls moved really well as they wandered around the stage, then on cue one girl goes and sets a deckchair up and sits down just as you would at the football or beach. Then it was my bit again.

On Yvette's signal I slipped out onto the stage and went over to the girl in the deckchair, and made out to try and chat her up, and then as we rehearsed I put my hand on her leg, and also as we rehearsed she got up to give me a make out girly slap on the cheek, and the crowd was all meant to laugh, and then we all go off.

It didn't quite happen like it did at rehearsal.

I put my hand on her leg, she got up and I don't know if she was nervous or what, but she nearly knocked my head off, and I almost buckled.

I can't remember anyone laughing.

I still don't think the crowd thought I was actually meant to be there.

Who is that bloke? Where's security?

The Lord Mayor came back on again and announced the successful design for that section and the winner came up and gave a speech. This gave everyone a few minutes to fly around and get into the next outfit, this time it was 'Evening Wear'.

The girls filed on to the stage again looking magnificent in the selection of beautiful flowing evening wear. This time Yvette's theme was a dinner party setting and I came onto the stage dressed as a waiter with a tray of champagne that the girls casually took, and pretended to sip.

They'd dressed me up in steel cap work boots, work shorts, and for the top half I had a dinner jacket and bow tie... and yes, I did look like a wanker.

This was probably the turning point in the show because now the crowd who'd only previously thought I possibly might be a wanker, now knew for certain I was one.

Yes, he's definitely part of the show, and he's a wanker.

No time to worry about it now, 'Sports Wear' was coming up fast. We'd not long hit backstage after the shame of Leisure Wear and Yvette rushed up with this outfit and told me what to do, I'm thinkin you gotta be joking! 'I wanted this bit to be really fresh and spontaneous' she told me, 'that's why I never mentioned it at rehearsal'.

Bloody hell, I wouldn't have turned up more likely.

No time for second thoughts, the Lord Mayor started his intro...

'Quick Phil, you're up first, don't forget the exercises'!

Onto the stage I went, and this time there was laughter, plenty of it.

I was wearing imitation cowhide trousers and a matching cowhide vest. The vest was open at the front highlighting my beer gut.

Then there were my fashion accessories.

In one hand I had a tennis racket and in the other I carried an esky. I headed down the catwalk and once I got to the end as per Yvette's instructions I put the esky down and went through a series of stretches and fake tennis shots. The fashion world pissed themselves, and it was about then I realised I might have to leave town for about six months till this one blew over.

I spun around picked up me esky and waddled off heading for the safety of backstage. Then the girls came out and completed Sports Wear and as usual, they looked stunning, then the presentation for the winner, a quick speech, and then a well deserved interval.

My role in the show so far couldn't be described as one of sophistication but to Yvette's credit she'd told me to bring my guitar, and as planned she let me go out and sing a few songs during the interval break.

Interval was really the break in the show where they served the three-course meal and the fashion 'Glitterazzi' got a chance to put the nosebag on. But it gave people a chance to see I wasn't a complete 'Tool' and I could sing a bit as well. I can't remember anyone taking any notice though.

I sung a few then left them with it, and went backstage and watched a few more girls adjust their underwear.

After interval we got back into it again.

I had to put me work boots, shorts, and dinner jacket outfit on again and escort girls around the stage for 'Glamour Wear', Yvette had a type of, Dad taking the daughter to her 'Debutant Ball' theme for this one.

The outfits and the models looked fantastic but I think I made a few people regurgitate the three course meal, and there was also plenty of hoots and chuckles coming from the crowd. Yvette's choreography and unique concept was winning everyone over, and I think most people were now really enjoying themselves.

After the winner's speech for Glamour Wear, a Drag Queen that Yvette had lined up went out and performed a song, and he was pretty good, he looked very feminine and he had a good act. I was talking to him earlier backstage and I congratulated him on his outfit, he reckoned it was because he had this 'good bitch' helping him, and the pretty offsider fussing away over

his hair just smiled. I mean if I tried to say something like that someone would probably call the bouncers and I'd be dragged out the back for being a smart arse. But it sounded really cool when he said it.

The Lord Mayor once again took the reins and introduced a few dignitaries and speeches were going left right and centre there for a while.

The big finale was coming up.

This was the big one; 'Bridal Wear', and the tension showed backstage. I was o.k. because I'd already firmly established myself as a 'Tosser' but the girl that I had to partner for the Bridal Wear section was not impressed.

I couldn't really blame her, the plan was for me and her to go walking out while they play the bridal waltz, and I've got a sign saying 'Just Married' on me back. It was all part of Yvette's show.

The fashion 'loser' slash 'wanker' finally has a win and gets a girl, and the show ends on a happy note.

Theoretically, it was a good idea, but the poor girl who took her modelling very seriously didn't want to have anything to do with me. She took offence to the thought of being connected with me, even though it was make believe, even though it was fantasy.

It was still too real.

Yvette had to really settle her down, and finally talked her into doing it, but the young glamour told Yvette if she has to do anything like this again she's going to give modelling away for good. It just wasn't worth the embarrassment she reckoned.

I suppose I wasn't cutting as fine a figure as I would have liked, but the outfits I had to wear didn't help much. She looked ravishing, and I looked like something that had just escaped from the Salvation Army.

The Lord Mayor pumped up the crowd a bit, the music started and out we strolled. The happy couple. We moved slowly towards the front of the stage and I did a bit of a turn revealing my 'Just Married' sign hanging on my back. This brought a heap of laughter from the part of the crowd that had sucked down a lot of Champagne and were into it, and appreciated the little twists Yvette had injected into the show.

Then there were the more conservative fashion boffins that just felt sorry for the girl.

Then I think there were still a few people wondering... who the hell is that bloke?

The music picked up and the rest of the models in their Bridal gear swanned out and there were some bloody great outfits, and the local designers deserve a pat on the back that's for sure. The Lord Mayor announced the winner for that category and then the overall winner of the night, and everyone that had anything to do with the show jumped on stage, danced around, and it was quite emotional.

What a night, and one very embarrassing night for the 'fashion loser' slash 'wanker', I just had to go live in another town for a while, that's all.

That was it for my modelling career though, no Major Success in this one, the offers never came flooding in from Paris or New York, not even Katherine or Mataranka.

Maybe one day, if they need someone to take the piss out of.

The Minor Success in all this was meeting Yvette because we're still friends these days. I thought she did a great job, and showed some real initiative and creativity pulling together the big awards the way she did, and she really is a class act.

I also got to see how hard the models work backstage and

the pressure they're under, always a fight against the clock. It was a real education for me.

A lot of blokes keep asking me what was it like?

You know, what was it like? And I say 'What was what like'?

And the conversation always gets onto me being backstage with all these beautiful girls getting dressed and undressed.

What was it really like?

Well, I usually sum it up in two words...

'Bloody Panoramic'!

TERRITORY TOUGH

A WHILE BACK I was there dreamily listening to the radio waiting for the news to come on, just kidding myself that I was up to date with politics and world affairs. I always like the news but to be completely honest most of the time it goes in one ear and out the other... but I tune in anyway.

This particular afternoon I'd tuned in a little early and the announcer was going on about the old saying 'Territory Tough'.

What's it mean? Where does it come from?

She carried on, appealing to her listeners to clarify the term.

From what I could gather the announcer hadn't been in the Northern Territory for long and she fair dinkum was looking for someone to describe what the term 'Territory Tough' was all about.

'Territory Tough'... I thought maybe I'd think about that for a bit.

Well, slowly the cogs started turning and I let my mind loosen up, images formed, and so I drifted for a while.

There I was collecting Crocodile eggs in a swamp in Arnhem Land.

Was that 'Territory Tough'?

No, I don't think so, it was just me doing a job no-one else wanted to do, it was just me trying to make a buck, and I was petrified the whole time. There was nothing tough about that.

What about the two blokes I ran into at a pub in Kakadu bragging about the metre long Barramundi they jerked out of the muddy South Alligator River, was that 'Territory Tough'? I wasn't sure.

Maybe the Road train drivers that carve their life on the highways and dirt tracks of the Territory's vastness. Were they Territory Tough? Could be, I suppose. It takes a lot of skill and resolve to jockey a Road train.

The news and weather crackled and came to an end and I'd missed the lot, deep in thought, I could barely hear the female announcer resume her show. My mind's meanderings had taken me back a little further, my eyes were shut but there was so much colour and excitement as my subconscious directed me to the place in time that held the answers.

It was Tanumbirini Station maybe ten years ago; I'd got a job as camp cook for a contract musterer by the name of Ben Tapp.

Ben Tapp was all cattle, nothing else in life mattered, with the exception of maybe horses and his family. Built like a Mack truck, he was born and bred for it.

One day we were all on the move, I'd gone up ahead of everyone else and was in the process of knocking up a damper and some Billy tea for smoko. Positioned up on a little stony hill overlooking the flat country around me I could see the mob of about 2,000 head being pushed along by Ben Tapp's team of young stockman. Ben himself was flying his helicopter working the lead, keeping the rogue Tanumbirini cattle heading in the right direction. Then all of a sudden Ben was right in amongst the mob flying low enough to kick up a great tornado of dust. He weaved in and out whipping the chopper around like it was a toy. With amazing skill he manoeuvred a grey Brahman Bull out of the mob using the skids of the chopper, perhaps only a metre or so above the ground.

Bit by bit he pushed it out and away from the herd.

The one-ton Brahman Bull knew the heat was on and made a run for it straight out across the flat. Ben dropped the chopper to the ground, was out of the cockpit in a flash, and was running full pelt after the Bull. As he ran Ben undid his belt, he caught up to the Bull who by now was breathing fire, Ben grabbed it by the tail and reefing it to the side threw the beast to the ground, and in a frenzy wrapped his belt around its back legs rendering the bull helpless.

Then casually big Ben Tapp pulled out his pocket knife and castrated the very irritated Bull.

It was all in a day's work as he then flew up and landed the chopper on top of the hill where I was. Shutting the machine down he strolled over to the campfire, a smile splashed across his face and without any inclination to brag or highlight what had just taken place asked me very humbly,

'Is the Billy boiled yet'?

Now, that's what I call Territory Tough!

Actually, it was probably a Minor Success the Billy was boiled, otherwise he probably would have flicked mine out as well.

Ben was the real deal all right. But there's so much more to this bloke than just being tough, and it would be a shame to end the story here.

Since the Tanumbirini days I've got to spend a fair bit of time with Ben and not many years go by where I don't work for him for a month or two.

A gifted leader of men, anyone that's ever worked for him is usually more than happy to work for him again. That is unless someone's done the wrong thing by him, and that usually results in the odd choking or drag through the dirt, but generally that's because they had it coming.

Ben has been known to vent his frustrations from time to time but that's all part of his rugged makeup as a cattleman, in a tough part of the country, taking on daily challenges that the average Australian only ever gets to read about. In his world he's had to be tough to survive, but Ben's done more than just that, he's carved out an empire for himself and his family and his extended family...the herd.

From the humble beginnings of contract mustering ten years ago, to now owning two prime cattle stations across the Top End, Mountain Valley and Maryfield. Ben's done it all without taking a backward step, and has still remained a pretty generous hearted bloke, in the true tradition of the outback Aussie.

Ben Tapp

But no-one likes the mechanics of a good deal better than he does, and under that rough and ready happy go lucky exterior is a bloke that is deep thinking and the cogs are constantly turning, observing, calculating, analysing and planning. Continually buying and selling stock, borrowing money, making money, land deals, horse sales, hardly a week goes by without Ben being involved in a transaction of some kind.

This is what sets him apart from a lot of his peers, Bens ability to sniff out and cook up a deal is finely tuned, and when it comes down to hard 'take no prisoners' business dealings, Ben Tapp is one of the most formidable blokes around and very rarely comes off second best.

Mountain Valley had not long been acquired by Ben and his family and it had been a big step for him. Formerly a cattle station of some repute the place was a little rundown and had been de-stocked. It was going to be a huge operation to get the place viable again, but if anyone could do it he could. He had the luxury of a very talented family though; his wife Traci and the three kids could handle themselves in all aspects of station work as well, and together they made a hard working team.

Ben had a plan and a vision for his family's future and it had taken all the business skill he had, to weave his way in, and secure the purchase of Mountain Valley.

Now he'd made it this far, a lot was hinging on the sale of their last much smaller property back near Katherine. If Ben got his asking price, albeit a slightly inflated one, his plan for the future and expansion as a cattleman looked promising and full of potential.

Somewhere across the sea an Indonesian entrepreneur that rated himself pretty highly in Indonesia as a mover and shaker was in the throws of empire building as well. He'd got wind of a good sizable chunk of land for sale in the Northern Territory on the Katherine River, great location, and great facilities. What an investment!

Money money money, profit profit profit; The Indonesian businessman's top lip curled back and gave a quiver as he picked up the scent of a possible money-spinner. He was sick of making money in Indonesia it was getting too easy, especially when you rubbed shoulders with royalty and government officials, not to mention politicians.

He was in the clique and he liked everyone to know it.

He looked down at the asking price on his Internet screen and laughed, he'd never paid anyone their asking price in his life, and you didn't have to be a 'Stonemason' to work out this bloke could really chisel.

His view of the Northern Territory was uneducated people

running around firing guns off in the main street. Australians aren't the sharpest tools in the shed he was thinkin, as a servant rushed over and topped up his teacup. The quick dealing Indonesian had made up his mind; this property would soon be his.

He'd fly down and reel who ever owned it in, just like a Barramundi, and then he'd apply the skills of his trade. He was the 'smiling assassin' when it came to real estate, and he had what ever it takes to take what you've got... all at the right price.

'Ha Ha Ha' he arrogantly chuckled, as a servant adjusted the pillow behind his head and passed him the telephone... 'ah, Mr Tapp.'

Ben placed the saddle over the rail and then hosed down the sweat caked on the young colt's back. The horse had a quiet nature and Ben was happy with the progress he was making with it. Gently he washed it down, keeping the animal's confidence in him.

'BEN... PHONE!' Came the scream from over at the home-stead.

'Bloody hell, doesn't anyone work anymore? All every bastard wants to do is talk on the bloody phone these days', Ben grumbled away to himself, as he reluctantly left the horse and made his way over to the Mountain Valley Homestead.

Snatching the phone from his wife he jammed it to his ear with one hand and tried to light a smoke with the other.

'Yeah, Ben Tapp here'...

'Ah Mr Tapp, Mr Tapp, how are you Mr Tapp' came the oriental sounding voice on the other end of the line.

'Ah Mr Tapp, Mr Tapp, I would be very interested in being interested in your land on Katherine River Mr Tapp, ah Mr Tapp'.

In a fraction of a second Ben's senses sharpened, the Marlborough Reds fell onto the floor as his eyes narrowed, and his back straightened.

The game had begun.

That initial phone call had left them both feeling pretty confident.

As far as the Indonesian was concerned Ben had played right into his hands by inviting him to come and spend a week with him on the property near Katherine.

The Indonesian would play the smiley little Asian card and let Ben think he was a pushover, and that's when your opponent is at the most susceptible, and he knew it. Then he planned to twist Ben's balls with the negotiations, thinking he was a hick.

Ben on the other hand was planning to really lay it on, he'd balloon the property up so much and make him think he was getting a bargain, then bluff the Asian into paying top dollar.

Of-course Ben would selectively leave out the bit about the wet season floods, no need to bore him with that information.

There was quite a bit at stake here for both men, Ben really needed to sell this Katherine River property to ease the financial burden on his purchase of Mountain Valley Station. Having to borrow a bit from the bank to get Mountain Valley, a good sale here could cover a lot of that debt.

On the other hand it was pride with the Indonesian, he always got what he wanted and he wanted this property... cheap.

The potential to gloat after purchasing a hunk of Australia physically excited him, and as far as he was concerned, his servants couldn't pack his suitcase fast enough.

Two top men in their fields were about to lock horns; it was really shaping up as a great contest of determination and guile. Almost on the scale of other great contests such as World Series Cricket or The Commonwealth Games, this was just as competitive.

This was International 'Deal or No Deal'.

Ben Tapp the bush hardened deep thinking cattleman, humble of heart and fists of iron was taking on one of the most successful wheeler dealers Indonesia had ever coughed up. Was he up to it? Could he keep his cool if the going got tough?

'Bloody hell Ben' Traci Tapp chipped away at her chain-smoking husband...' Bloody hell not another one.'

Ben had been lighting one after the other the whole three hour drive from Mountain Valley over to the Katherine River property. Traci's lungs were screaming for mercy, a non-smoker, she felt like she'd just been through 'Ash Wednesday'. Ben was nervous. In the three days since the phone call he'd gone way out of his way on this deal. He'd downloaded some Indonesian words and recipes off the Internet, and he had Traci all geed up to cook some genuine Indonesian food. Ben also had downloaded some traditional Indonesian music and had it on a C.D ready to go.

Ben Tapp was weaving a web.

He wanted this bloke to feel relaxed, he wanted this bloke to feel like he was back home in Jakarta, he wanted this bloke to reach in his pocket and pull out some top dollar, and if Ben Tapp had to wear a sarong as well, he'd bloody do it. The scene was set.

The hire car pulled up just before lunch and out stepped the Indonesian.

With Traci by his side Ben extended a warm handshake

'Boy, have I got a deal for you!'

and a genuine Indonesian greeting that he'd got off the Internet and had been practising. Neither himself, Traci, or the Indonesian understood what he said.

It didn't matter.

The contest had begun and the wheels of the deal were in motion, it was early days, too early for anyone to show much emotion. Just casual chatter with both parties foxing, trying to get an insight into the make up of the other.

The Indonesian was slick, he was short and wiry with oily black hair that went back in waves across his head, and his teeth had more gold in them than what was being pulled out of Broken Hill. His eyes constantly went from left to right, as if he was expecting an ambush.

But he was taking it all in; every tree, every brick, every fence post, his mind working overtime, adding subtracting calculating, all hidden behind a constant smile.

Traci had prepared a great little lunch, curry and rice with everyone all very chipper. The Indonesian's English was reasonably good so there was plenty of chat. Strategies even at this early stage were already being played out, the Indonesian constantly bringing up the fact he had a great relationship with all the top people in Indonesia, and he was very connected and very successful. He repeated this like a mantra, trying to impress the Tapps and get the high ground.

Ben felt like kicking him up the arse taking his wallet and telling him to beat it. If there was any thing he hated it was a 'big noter'. But there was too much at stake, and he had to stay cool and keep sharp, 'stay in the saddle' he kept telling himself 'stay in the bloody saddle'.

That afternoon Ben took him for a drive around some of the property, he decided to play one of his trumps straight up, and so he slid his special Indonesian C.D into the player. Ben who was a Slim Dusty man from way back thought it was the worst thing he'd ever heard, but smiled and tried to hum along. 'Dang ding doong dang do dong ding' went the traditional Indonesian music. The Indonesian's head rocked from left to right and his gold plated smile lit up the Toyota, 'ah Mr Tapp this is beautiful Mr Tapp', and off they went across the paddock.

Ben wasn't enjoying this, he really wasn't.

It was the first time Ben had sung along with traditional Indonesian music and he hoped it would be his last, but it was all part of the process, all part of the mission to get this bloke to pay the asking price.

As long as the Indonesian's arse pointed to the ground he had no intentions of paying the asking price, not in a blue fit, he never did.

If Ben knew that, he might have played it different, but Ben was giving it his all, he was going above and beyond the call of duty, he was really extending himself. The Indonesian was made of money and that's all that Ben needed.

Coming across some lush grassy country on a good bit of black soil plain Ben went into raptures about the quality of the native grass and its potential to fatten cattle, he laid it on thick, as if he'd personally grazed on it himself and could thoroughly recommend it.

The Indonesian was impressed, 'ah Mr Tapp, fat cattle much money Mr Tapp, ah Mr Tapp my friends very happy if I buy property Mr Tapp'.

Ben Tapp smiled, lit one up, got a lungful, and started to feel he was getting somewhere. 'Stay in the saddle' he told himself 'stay in the bloody saddle...we've almost got him'.

Over the next few days the arm wrestle intensified.

Ben had gone on to balloon all aspects of the property; he'd even started on the water quality in the river.

'You could bottle the bastard'! He reckoned.

As far as Ben was concerned this was a dream property, it could even be developed as a tourism venture as well, 'I'm just turning them away every day, its just like bloody Disney-land here sometimes' Ben reckoned.

The Indonesian's excitement rising with each one of Ben's claims.

If we checked out the scoreboard at this stage it showed Ben Tapp thinking he was in a pretty solid position. He'd really put in the hard yards, he'd fed him up on the right sort of tucker, he'd made him feel very comfortable, and was the perfect host, and he'd done a great job highlighting the potential of the property. Now that the time had come to talk money Ben felt pretty good, he'd got the Indonesian bloke where he wanted him.

He dropped his old-fella out, took a mighty drag on his smoke and had a well deserved leak out on the front lawn.

It had been a hard week, but Ben was quietly confident.

At times he'd almost lost it, his temper had almost got the better of him, but there was no need Ben mused, slow and steady wins the race every time, I mose well get ready to count the money he was thinkin.

Around the other side of the house, the Indonesian had just got off his mobile phone after telling one of his government official mates back home, that he had this cowboy where he wanted him. He'd done a lot of smiling, and Ben had done a lot of talking, and that's exactly what he'd planned.

Dropping out his Indo old-fella, he also had a well deserved leak around the side of the house, breathing in the sweet eucalyptus scented outback air, as he marked out his potential territory.

The cocky little businessman was in no doubt; he'd get this one cheap.

Next morning they were all up bright and early, Traci knocked up a tasty Indonesian Omelette and the day was full of promise.

Ben handed the Indonesian bloke a coffee and suggested they sit outside in the sun and talk a bit of turkey.

'It's been great having you here mate, but let's sort this thing out, hopefully you've seen enough of the place by now, you ready to dot the I's and cross the T's or what?'

'Oh yes Mr Tapp, let's deal Mr Tapp', then he took a slurp from his coffee and gave one more 'Ah Mr Tapp'... just for effect.

Ben played it straight down the line.

'You know me asking price, she's a good property, so you bloody in or what'? Then Ben leant back in his chair and sucked the guts out of a Marlborough Red.

The Indonesian smiled that broadly Ben thought he was going to dislocate his jaw.

Then after a bit more head nodding and a shake of hands the deal was done. What an anticlimax. Ben couldn't believe it; he thought there'd be at least a bit of haggling. Must have done a good job promoting the place, I knew he couldn't say no, Ben was thinking.

With the deal done the Indonesian feller was keen to get back home and resume his very important life mixing with very important people, and he once again big noted himself. This time it didn't worry Ben much, he was too happy and he even made out to be a bit impressed.

'I will organise the payment and formalities straight away Mr Tapp as soon as I get back', no worries mate replied a beaming Ben.

After a quick coffee and a few mobile phone calls organising flights etc the Indonesian threw his bags in the hire car and said his goodbye.

Ben tried to repeat a traditional Indonesian farewell he got off the Internet and had been practising. He tried, but neither himself, Traci, or the Indonesian understood what he'd just said.

It didn't matter - the deal was done.

That night Ben and Traci celebrated in Kirby's Back Bar in Katherine, Ben had a few and fired up a bit, 'I told you Traci that C.D would do the trick, you should have seen him when I cranked it up, the poor bastard just went weak'.

'I was even bloody singing along!'

'Dang ding doong dang do dong bloody ding dang' went Ben, staggering around pretending to sing some traditional Indonesian, and spilling rum and coke all over the people next to him. It was a well deserved celebration for him and Traci, and a very timely sale of the property.

Next day, once the hangover lifted Ben and Traci were keen to get back to Mountain Valley and see how everything was going, and share the good news.

Somewhere across the sea, in a very palatial abode, one very happy Indonesian businessman sat back, rubbed his hands together, and laughed.

He was no mug.

The seasoned real estate warrior had put a hook in Ben's mouth, and was getting ready to reel him in. He very much liked the Katherine River property, and yes, he had planned to follow through with the deal, but there'd be a twist. He was going to play a game he'd played so many times before, and successfully.

Reading between the lines he knew Ben needed to sell this place to cover his arse on the acquisition of Mountain Valley, Ben never let on, but a few strategic questions in-between playing the goofy Asian, gave him enough to piece the scenario together.

If he could stall Ben for another four or five weeks and fox on the payment, Ben would be that little bit more desperate, then he'd make up a story about having unseen financial problems come up, and that's when he'd offer to renegotiate and get Ben's asking price down.

Ben would be susceptible, and possibly might unload the property a fair bit cheaper, just to get his hands on the working capital he needed.

The game was well and truly still on, and it was just starting to heat up.

'BEN... PHONE!' Came the scream from across at the homestead.

'Bloody hell' grumbled Ben, 'can't a bloke break in a bloody horse in bloody peace, mose well buy a bloody pushbike and ride that bastard'...

'YOU TAKE IT TRACI!'

'Ah Mrs Traci, Mrs Traci, much business here, very much important, sorry for delay' went the oriental voice, 'my friends very important we very busy, I fix business soon', and then he gave a quick, 'Ah Mrs Traci' for effect, and then hung up.

Traci immediately walked over to the yards and conveyed the message to Ben, who'd just been bucked off the colt and was laying face down in the dirt. Not feeling that talkative.

Across the sea the smiling business man hung up the phone and took another wrap with his handline as he reeled the Tapps in just that little bit more. Indonesians are traditionally very warm people, and he wasn't a bad man, he was just a business man, and this little manoeuvre was all in a day's work.

Later in the week the phone rang at Mountain Valley and it was a repeat performance from the Indonesian with Traci taking the call, as Ben was out flying his helicopter checking cattle.

When Ben returned Traci passed on the message and her concerns, Ben told her to give the bloke a fair go, and the business man across the sea took another wrap on the hand-line. Three days later the same again, this time Ben was out fencing, and once again he told Traci to relax.

Another wrap went on the Indonesian's handline, and he wondered if Mr Tapp could feel the hook in his mouth.

He had big plans for the river property, and a few of his rich high rolling Indonesian friends were keen to get in on it as well, another couple of weeks, keep stalling, keep playing the game.

The funny thing is, with anyone else he probably would have almost got away with it.

Ben Tapp was up with the sun and launched straight into his usual routine of walking out onto the lawn to drop out his old-fella, have a leak, then light up a smoke. Then it was breakfast, which consisted of another seven Marlborough Reds and a cup of strong coffee. As Ben went through this morning ritual his thoughts would automatically go into an assessment of the day ahead, and any circumstance that concerned him.

Like a computer his deep thinking mind would work through all the files, analysing his family's situation, his business dealings, his future prospects, his cattle, and all other

Ben Tapp inhaling a hearty breakfast.

things that affected the direction his life would take. Like I said earlier in this story, there was a lot more to Ben Tapp's make-up than just being tough. His moves in life were always well thought out. He knew that deal with the Indonesian went too well, it was all too easy, and his intuition had alerted him to the fact.

But Ben chose not to take notice that particular time.

It felt so good to think the property would be sold so quickly and for such a good price, it fitted into his plans so well. For once he didn't have to struggle for it and bust his guts getting something, for once something fell into his lap.

Now it was time to follow his intuition again, that same intuition that had served him so well over his life, that same gifted intuition that had got him and his family through so many scrapes and given them a future.

A hot flush went through his body and his teeth bit down hard on his latest Marlborough Red as the formulations of his mind came to a hot blooded conclusion...

'That Bastard's been playin me'.

The blood running through Ben's veins started to heat, and he rushed for another smoke. He walked down to the yards to check on the colt, giving himself a chance to calm down and think rationally. But it was no good.

He looked around and took in the scene at Mountain Valley, there was so much work to do and such a big future to be had, there was no room for shades of grey, life had to be black and white.

There was only one way to play it, and that was Ben Tapp's way.

Ben resembled a steam train as strode out across the flat heading for the homestead; puffs of smoke rising up at regular intervals from a half sucked Marlborough as he wound up a bit of speed and got a good stride up.

The look on his face suggested anyone or anything getting between him and wherever he was going, could be very dangerous.

He reached the homestead, grabbed the phone with a vice like grip, and proceeded to make a long distance phone call.

Somewhere across the sea in a luxurious home in Indonesia a phone rang.

'It's still time for sleep, who would be ringing now?' The businessman mumbled, as a servant rushed the phone to his bedside.

On the line was one of the fiercest sounding voices he'd ever heard.

'Put the money in the bank or FUCK OFF'.

Ben Tapp waited for a reply... but the phone line went dead.

The game was over.

'Put the money in the bank or FUCK OFF!'

THE PIG

CAN'T REALLY REMEMBER why I was going or what the reason was.

Sometimes there isn't one.

Usually there isn't one.

I was in Katherine packing the Toyota for a trip down to Alice Springs or maybe some place beyond. A mate pulled up and asks me if I could give his girlfriend a lift to this Aboriginal community somewhere west of the one horse town of 'Ti-tree,' on my way through to the 'Alice'.

I said no worries; a bit of company won't kill me I'm thinkin.

It was a great trip down the track, a few good campfires, some good chat with me mate's girlfriend 'Anna' and a couple of days and 1000 kms later we left the smooth bitumen of the Stuart Highway, and headed in on a dirt track for the community.

The country looked like it was just coming off the back of a good season, but now drying off a bit. We passed through some really pretty red ochred hills, laced with sage green clumps of Spinifex, and then on to some open grassy plains, at times busy with Bush Turkey and Kangaroos.

It was a pleasant 150k or so and although the track wasn't

real flash there was nothing that was going to stop us.

The community was nestled on the edge of an inland river, which was bone dry, but easy on the eye, with its commanding Gum lined banks and white rippling sandy riverbed.

This was home to the 'Warlpiri' people, a strong minded resolute tribe of Indigenous desert dwellers that have survived the challenges put before them for many thousands of years. For me it was a great opportunity to go someplace I'd never been before and as we drove in and saw the friendly faces, I felt like sticking around a bit.

Everyone was looking forward to meeting Anna, and they were excited when we finally rocked up.

Anna's job was to help the women with their silk screening project in the hope that one day it could become a viable little business for them. The local women had all the talent in the world, but they just needed a bit of a kick off. This is where Anna and her experience was gunna be handy.

We hadn't been there long when Anna decided to check out the old house that was going to be used as the women's art centre. On inspection it was pretty dilapidated and it definitely needed a bit of work to get it up to scratch. So Anna reckons can I stay for a while and help fix the old building up a bit. A couple of Aboriginal blokes reckoned the local council could give me a few bucks if I helped out, which was really nice of them, and I think they could see I wasn't in a hurry to go anywhere, so I agreed to stay and do a bit.

After yarning it up for a while they took us over to our accommodation, a nice roomy house on the edge of the community, and we were sharing with three schoolteachers.

It was a good set up and everyone was very friendly.

The kettle got put on and there we are, all sitting around, and I see something out the corner of my eye flash past the window. Then a few minutes later it flashed past again.

What was that? I'm thinkin?

It was too big to be a dog and it was really motoring.

Then again... and again!

What ever the thing is, it was circling the house, but the curtains were half drawn so I still couldn't make out what it was. I was gunna say something, then all of a sudden there's this humungous 'Bang' 'Bang' 'Bang' on the back door.

Everyone sprung up.

'Oh no not that Bastard again' says one of the schoolteachers.

'He's after that bloody horse feed again the Bastard'!

'Bang' 'Bang' on the back door, so we all go to the back window and outside is a crazy looking pig holding a chair in its mouth, and bashing it against the back door of the house!

Was this normal?

I don't think so.

There was a pig with a chair in its mouth.

'Piss off you Bastard' yelled the schoolteacher and although she looked feminine enough she could really handle herself when it come to colourful language.

'Drop the chair and Fuck off you bacon coated prick', she commanded.

The pig spun around wildly a couple of times, dropped the chair, and trotted off in the direction of the dry river bed, stopping every so often to look back and give the crowd at the back window a real evil beady eyed look of disdain.

'One of these days pig' yelled the school teacher, 'one of these friggen days'.

Well, I'm thinkin - if this isn't the most bizarre thing I've ever witnessed, it's definitely gotta be up there.

What sort of pig was this anyway?

The schoolteacher swore on for a little bit longer, and then with the kettle boiled we sat back down with a cup of tea.

I didn't want to appear like a bloke that had never seen crazy stuff before, I didn't want to appear naïve, or out of my depth, but I had to get some answers, so I very casually took a sip from my tea and reckoned 'What's the story with the pig'?

Off went the five foot two very feminine schoolteacher-swearing machine,

'That piece of Pork Crackling Shit'! She started up.

'One of these days I'm going to cut its bastard head off and use it as a bloody door stop, if only the community would let me'.

This was getting interesting, and without much more prompting from me she let loose with the whole amazing story.

One of the Aboriginal families had somehow got the pig when it was just a piglet; they thought it would make a good pet. As it got older it started to go crazy, like it was possessed or something, and it started killing the other pet dogs and stuff. It kept growing and now it was terrorizing the whole community. The pig was totally out of control, but the Aboriginal people didn't want to kill it, because if it was this crazy when it was in an earthly form, imagine how much worse it could get if it got to be a spirit.

Who knows what powers it would have then?

The pig had previously got into the school teacher's house when they were away and tore apart the sacks of horse feed they kept in there. It trashed the place so now the teachers had their own vendetta to settle with the pig as well.

So as crazy as it sounds for one reason or another the pig was running this place, it was the pig's town...and the pig was a bastard.

Next morning I set to work on the women's art centre chipping away with my very limited handyman skills, but I was determined to make a difference. I'd forgot about the pig briefly when about mid morning there was a big 'Willy Willy' wind out on the flat.

It picked up bits of old corrugated iron and spun them around and much dust got funnelled high up in the air in a spiralling clatter. The Willy Willy danced for a while, then slowly ran out of wind and the dust and debris settled back down again.

This was the cue for the pig to make his entrance.

The pig must have had a flare for the theatrical, and through a veil of dust he'd emerge. Trotting arrogantly, head swaying from side to side, and beady eyes glaring with a sinister glow. I'd never seen anything quite like it and I stopped and watched it trot past.

Dogs were cowering away in the shadows trying to keep out of its way. The pig owned the streets and was completely fearless.

He went through the community like a dose of Epsom salts.

He knocked over all the rubbish bins, routed up any green lawn he could find and basically pillaged whatever it could. I even saw it pushing this tap with its snout till it finally came on and it got a drink. After terrorizing the community it would trot back down to its lair somewhere in the dry riverbed. Everyday was much the same; about mid morning you'd get that Willy Willy coming through, and out would emerge the pig.

I suppose I'd been there a couple of weeks working away and as per usual walked back across to the school teacher's house for a bit of lunch around midday. Things were pretty normal; in a really bizarre freaky way, it was just another day.

Earlier I'd seen the pig trotting out of town heading for his home near the gates of hell down in the riverbed. He'd done his marauding for the day, and was obviously gunna chill out for the arvo.

We were all on the back veranda having a sandwich and could see the tell tale dust cloud of a vehicle coming in our direction. There wasn't a lot of traffic into the community due to its isolation, so everyone was keen to see who it was. About a quarter of an hour later a Toyota Tray back pulls up, and out jumps this bloke dressed in cowboy gear, complete with ten gallon hat. He obviously knew one of the school-teachers, the one that swore a lot. She greeted him with, 'You still pushin that pen you ugly bastard?'

She was sweet and petite, but I'd like a dollar for every time I heard her swear.

Anyway the bloke dressed like a cowboy actually came out from town on Social Security business. He was an office worker but just dressed country.

On the back of his vehicle stood two mean looking Staghound dogs. They were shiny and in good condition, obviously he was very proud of them as he reached up and gave them a pat.

'Fuckin pan lickers are lookin good' says the teacher.

'Yeah, you should see what they do to a bloody Kangaroo' replied the Social Security bloke, with a sense of pride.

'No Bullshit' replied the hard swearing schoolteacher, and so the banter continued for a minute or two.

Then, as if appearing out of thin air like an apparition, standing ten metres away, staring beady eyed and crazy was... 'The Pig'.

No one saw him approach. No one saw anything.

It was just there.

Its stare fixed firmly on the Toyota tray back, and the two Staghounds.

This town belonged to the pig, and as far as the pig was concerned, I don't think he remembered sending out invitations to two Staghounds. The Social Security guy turned and saw the pig the same time his schoolteacher friend yelled 'There's that feral bastard of a bastard pig'!

Well, the Social Security guy couldn't resist, I could see he had a soft spot for the teacher and rockin up with his big hunting dogs on the back of the rig was a mighty cool look, and now out of nowhere a pig turns up. I think he thought all his Christmases had just come at once. This was a great opportunity to show off, and he wasn't gunna miss it.

He turned to the pair of snarling Staghounds and gave the command 'Get hold of that pig'!

You could have heard a pin drop.

I mean, everyone hated the pig, but did we really want to see him torn apart right in front of our very eyes.

Did it have to end this way for the pig?

The hounds lunged off the back of the Tray back, lips curled back with hate, teeth gleaming in the midday glare.

They were bred to kill and they revelled in delight once their owner gave the command. The hounds flew for the pig with an unbridled bloodlust, and I was all set to go inside and finish my sandwich and then come out later and bury the pig. I didn't need to witness the kill.

But hang on, the pigs up on his tippy toes like a ballet dancer, and he's spinning around like a top at incredible speed. One minute he's spinning clockwise, then he'd spin anti clockwise! The dogs circled him wildly but they couldn't get an opening to get in and grab it. Then with blistering speed the pig lunged out and grabbed one of the hounds by the throat, and drove it into the dust with all its bodyweight.

The hound was suffocating as the pig tightened its grip. The other dog kept barking and stuff but with its mate out of the fight he wasn't game to go too close. As the last bit of air was being choked out of the hound the panic bells were struck by the Social Security bloke.

'Someone get the pig off!' He was yelling.

'Get the pig off' 'Get the pig off'!

I obviously was never destined to finish my sandwich in peace so I got up and turned the hose on and squirted the pig. The pig threw the dog about five meters and swaggered off in the direction of the dry river bed, and once again stopped a few times to look back with his beady demonic gaze, then trotted arrogantly away to his lair.

The pig had won the day and there was no denying it, this was not your average pig.

'Mother Fucker' declared the saintly looking schoolteacher, 'Mother Fucker', she repeated, and then she spat and grinded the green globule into the dust with her thong clad foot.

'Did you see that porker spin'! She reckoned.

The Social Security bloke scooped up his dog and laid him in the back of the tray back. I don't think it was quite dead but it wasn't real alive either. He was physically shaken just like its owner, but you can't hold it against a bloke for trying to show off in front of the chicks. He just picked the wrong pig.

So he drove off with his one and a half dogs and went about finishing his business over at the council office. Minding his business in the first place might have saved him some embarrassment, but I must admit, it was great lunchtime entertainment. A lot of people would have paid good money to see a pig spin around like a ballet dancer, then choke a dog.

The pig was definitely possessed, demonic crazy and also had a lot of other issues as well, but it could turn on a good show that's for sure. I was wondering if anything so gung-ho as the pig would reach old age. One thing for sure it wouldn't be going into anyone's camp oven without a fight.

I stayed on a few more weeks till the old house started to take shape and Anna was happy with it, then it was time to hit the track.

It had been a great experience living in that community and when I told everyone I was going, the Aboriginal mob thought they'd score a Minor Success at my expense.

They wanted me to catch the pig and take it with me, and get it the hell out of there.

I'm thinking, you got to be joking.

So to completely avoid the issue I left the next morning before the sun and before anyone was awake. No way was I putting the pig in my vehicle, I could just see it, once the bastard saw how to drive and change the gears and stuff, he probably would have pushed me out the door, and roared off in me Toyota.

It definitely was not your average pig.

THE POWER OF DAMPER

NOW TIMES WERE GETTING TOUGH in an already tough life. You come home one day and you find out your wife's done you wrong, and your girlfriends done you even wronger. It's not looking good.

You're at the end of the line and the ceiling of life is caving in bit-by-bit and chunk-by-chunk. You know deep down its time for something spiritual to enter your life, sustenance for a hungry soul.

You knew it was always gunna come to this - a pilgrimage - a journey to the place where all spiritual roads and highways meet, the essence of life, the crusty inner sanctum of consciousness.

Or in other words... 'The Damper'.

The miles melt away behind you as you thump along the track in a very willing 1988 Diesel Toyota and a feeling of well-being almost intoxicates you and rolls over you like a wave, and the 8 cans of beer you've already sucked down are gently rattling around on the floor, caressing the moment.

The shackles of a life hard fought slowly release their iron grip as you crack a can and go careering off the road to avoid a dead wallaby. You come to a grinding skidding halt, for this is the place of your destiny, your fate.

After regaining consciousness you're not quite sure how you got there, as you crack can number ten, but there's no time to waste.

It's time for the Damper making ceremony.

A fire is lit and with the mixing bowl facing the holy city of 'Tamworth' you proceed to mix up the sacred sod. Flour and water humbly transforming itself. With the patron saint of damper Slim Dusty crooning country hymns from the ghetto blaster, the damper is placed in the camp oven, and two or three shovel fulls of coals are placed around, under, and on top of the camp oven, and the ceremony is complete.

One hour later the damper is miraculously transformed into a golden orb.

How this happens we will never understand?

A can is instantly cracked and skulled followed by a huge slab of hot crusty damper, dripping with desire, and also golden syrup. Slim Dusty chants faster and faster, louder and

louder, Slims rhythms intoxicating as you sink your teeth into the dampers glorious dough.

It's just too much, for man is only flesh and blood and so you pass out curled up in the dirt... you've been moved.

Now, once again as an empty beer can rolls past your snoring scone, you're at one with the universe, for you've been touched... by the 'POWER OF DAMPER'.

CHINA MEETS ARNHEM LAND

WELL THERE I WAS, another beautiful dry season morning in August, everything was rolling along nicely. I'd picked up some work helping this friend renovate his house and I was doing my duty pressure cleaning the concrete driveway with this high-pressure water blasting apparatus.

I was going my hardest when all of a sudden I got this vibrating feeling in my side pocket... it was my new mobile phone.

Over the hum of the water blaster I could hear the earthy tones of an old tour guide acquaintance 'Jungle Jacky'.

'We need a camp cook' she reckoned.

'Ten days in Arnhem Land with this Chinese film mob can you make it?'

'When are you leaving?' I asked.

'NOW!'

'Let me think about it' I told her.

Ten seconds later I said to the friend I was working for I'll be back in ten days, and I took off. I raced home grabbed me swag and a few clothes and headed for the shed where we were all meeting. I wasn't gunna miss this one, and I don't mind being a little spontaneous every so often.

I'd come across Jungle Jacky a few times when I worked as a tour guide and she was a good operator and nice to be around, so there was no need to think about it too deeply.

When I got to the shed the expedition was ready to roll, several four wheel drives, an 8 ton truck loaded to the hilt and of course the twenty five or so Chinese. This was no ordinary bunch of snap happy visitors either; this was an elite media group from an emerging world super power. There were internationally acclaimed photographers, journalists, writers, and a core group of professionals from China's main television network. Their aim it seemed was to produce a documentary style television program focussing on nature and culture entitled 'Journey into a Mystery Land'. The program, which will screen to a potential Chinese audience of several million viewers, hoped to feature western Arnhem Land, Kakadu National Park and Uluru.

Jungle Jacky was the head guide on the trip and what an ambassador she was. A very giving caring person, Jungle Jacky has a heart the size of a Bull Buffalo, and a smile that could kick start a tractor.

She was Mother Teresa wrapped in Khaki.

The rest of the support crew was made up of Jungle Jacky's brother Ben, two pommy backpackers Zoe and Tom and a skinny but happy go lucky truck driver called 'Bulk'. What a team we all made as the convoy snaked its way into a service station on the outskirts of Darwin to fuel up. It was diesel and ice coffee all around – then a little unexpected trouble struck.

A passing transport inspector threw the book at one of the trailers we were towing. After a gaggle of mobile phone calls someone reckoned another trailer was on its way, could we wait an hour?

Well, it didn't faze the Chinese film crew they sprung into action taking film after film of the defected trailer, and then they filmed Jungle Jacky standing next to the trailer, and then they forgot about the trailer, and just filmed Jungle Jacky.

This mob had come to film and they were going to film... everything.

A lot of the Chinese had worked in war torn areas around the world so one grumpy- arse transport inspector wasn't going to faze them.

Finally the convoy rolled on, complete with new trailer, the old one pushed into the corner of the fuel station car park, and left alone like a primary school kid in the playground that no one liked.

We swung east off the Stuart Highway travelling for a few hours, and then a short lunch stop at the South Alligator River.

In my role as camp cook I thought I'd jam a few sandwiches into them, but according to the Chinese translator that was travelling with us they don't much like bread and they won't eat cheese.

I don't know where she got that from, they proceeded to eat just about all the cheese we had, they circled the blocks of 'Farmland semi-matured' like sharks, all that was left was a bit of the plastic, and when it came to bread, if you got between them and the loaf it was outright dangerous.

The Chinese liked their tucker.

We left the muddy South Alligator with a full tank and the camera shutters were already smokin thanks to a few Wallabies and a Kookaburra, and by mid afternoon we crossed the mighty East Alligator River into the cultural treasure trove of Arnhem Land, and wound our way through some fantastic country.

Rugged escarpments housing rock art and stories dating back to the Dreamtime. Wetlands teaming with bird life, and

the Aboriginal community of Gunbalanya proudly keeping a watchful eye on one of the most culturally significant places in the world. Just like the cheese, the Chinese digested it all with great excitement.

We followed a badly corrugated track on a few more hundred kilometres till we reached the coast, about half way up towards Coburg Peninsular.

Our first camp was on a beach so pretty it just about made a grown man break down and weep.

The Arnhem Land coast is so serene, with its soft colours and untouched features. The Casuarina trees grow up to the high tide mark, and just set off the tranquillity. Their shade makes a gentle whistling tune as the sea breeze passes through the needle shaped foliage. Green blue waters caressing the soft white sand, all splashed in tropical sunlight.

Even the crocodiles seemed relaxed.

It had been a tremendous day's travel, no breakdowns or blowouts but poor old Bulk bogged the truck just before the beach, which caused a little bit of a drama, but once the tents and swags were organised I drove a sausage sizzle into them and I think the Chinese slept like babies. I don't reckon the Chinese translator ever had the pleasure of a sausage sizzle before, and I explained that this dish plays a major role in our dietary development as Aussies. Once babies outgrow the breast they usually hook straight on to a fat laden snag. All up it's probably our national dish, I pointed out.

She was fascinated.

I was just so thankful Jungle Jacky had thought of me with the camp cook job, because I felt I was getting bogged down a bit in town. I could feel my batteries charging up now that I was back out bush where I belonged.

Over the next few days the Aboriginal family that lived on that stretch of beach proved very hospitable and they enjoyed sharing their paradise with the Chinese. Aboriginal people are gifted teachers, and they really took the visitors under their wing. The Chinese responded by openly appreciating every great moment. They were invited to share in some ceremony, hunting, bush tucker and some quality time around the campfire.

I couldn't believe what a diverse group we all were, but yet everyone hit it off so well. It makes me think maybe more people should get off their arse and have these types of inter-actions with people from other cultures.

Here's a mob from Beijing sitting around a campfire with a mob of Arnhem Land Aboriginal people, and they're really harmonizing.

I couldn't help but feel that maybe there is some hope for people around the world to get on with each other; just some-how we've got to get through the bullshit. Anyway, our little multicultural mob on the beach was doing just fine.

My day as cook was starting around five in the morning under the stars, the best time of the day. The first job was to get a good fire going and boil plenty of water for tea. The Chinese loved to drink this green tea stuff, and it wasn't just a teabag in a cup, they'd shove half the bush into a pannikin and then add water. She was a wild looking brew, but the Chinese have been around for thousands of years so they know what's good for them and what works, it actually wasn't a bad drop. Then I'd boil a heap of eggs and put out some Corn Flakes and milk, and that was pretty much breakfast. The Chinese didn't muck around, they mixed the eggs in with the Corn Flakes and tucked into it.

Obviously their eating habits and what they eat is totally different from ours, but to their credit they never complained, and they ate whatever was put in front of them.

Some mornings I'd make toast on the coals and put out some marmalade and a heap of scrambled eggs and they'd mix all that together as well.

Probably one of me best creations came out one evening. I had some marinated chicken and I was gearing up to barbeque it, but on advice from the Chinese translator she reckoned just put it all in a big pot of boiling water. My first reaction was doubtful, but I did it, and bugger me it was O.K. The chicken was really moist and tender and the marinade went into the water and made a really tasty soup.

After that feed I reached legend status. Everyone wanted to know the recipe. I could have gone straight to Beijing and opened me own restaurant.

Each day the friendships grew, and although the language barrier was hard everyone was getting better at communicating in their own special ways. One young Chinese girl was just so taken by the beauty of the place she couldn't take the smile

Jungle Jacky checking out my kitchen.

off her face, and she'd come up and giggle and touch you a bit, and smile and giggle a bit more. It was just her way of saying 'hey mate I'm having a bloody good time here'.

I couldn't pronounce her Chinese name but translated into English her nickname was 'Little Fatty', but it should have been 'Little Spunky', because she was very attractive, and in the words of the late great king of rock and roll Elvis Presley, she was just a hunka hunka burnin love.

Another character was a bloke called Alex Wu, back in Beijing he is a radio announcer and has a popular show that millions of people listened to religiously, I suppose you could say he was the John Laws of China. He could speak a little English and for someone so popular he was very humble. His

Little Fatty

job was to call Beijing and give reports of the trip live on radio, but I didn't like his chances of finding a phone around here. He had a good sense of humour though, and it was good chewing the fat with him about living in Beijing, and this was the first time in his life he had camped out, so there was much to discuss about our two different worlds.

A bloke called Lou-Man was one of the main blokes running the show and he seemed pretty capable. He'd spent a fair bit of time in Sydney as well and I think he really took to the Aussie culture, anyway he could swear like one. He had a tremendous amount of energy and I think that helped in bringing everyone together so well.

One of the Photographers on the trip was a lady called 'Zi', and I'm sure that's not how you spell it but that's how it sounded. She was in the thick of everything, formerly a Major in the Chinese military she was also very pleasant company, and I wonder what sights she would have seen in her life.

One other lady grabbed my attention and I wouldn't even try to pronounce her name but she was so sweet and friendly, like a breath of fresh air every time she came around my camp-fire. I really enjoyed extending the hand of friendship to her, but would have liked to extend the friendship a bit further, but I stayed professional.

I'm sure she didn't come all the way over to Australia just to get mauled by the old mangy camp cook.

We stayed at our camp on the beach for about three days, but I could have stayed another three years, it was so nice.

Then the convoy packed up and we rolled away from the coast. We took on the corrugation again, and rattled our way back through the escarpment country and into the Aboriginal community of Gunbalanya. Once again the Aboriginal people were very hospitable, and shared their home with the Chinese film mob. We spent a very rewarding few days around there and the Chinese got treated to some very special ceremonial stuff, and feasted on rock art dating back tens of thousands of years.

I think the Chinese mob being an old culture as well, could really relate to the strong connections the Aboriginal people share with their land. The rock art on the overhangs and rock faces through that area is unbelievable.

Such intricate figures and designs that represent such powerful meaning and prophecy. Lessons and stories, and thousands of years of cultural evolution, all documented in ochre, seared into the sandstone for eternity.

Through appropriate ceremony, the local Aboriginal people

are constantly regenerating themselves and the spirit in the living things, and the country around them. As one old Aboriginal elder was giving a talk about the significance of the area, and the problems Aboriginal people face these days as the twenty first century sweeps through their ancient culture, one of the support crew Ben, just broke down in tears.

Ben was a big strapping bloke but he was a bit sensitive as well, and I think he must have really picked up on the spirit and power of this area, and the genuine feelings the old Aboriginal bloke shared.

This trip wasn't just proving to be an eye opener for the Chinese mob; it was also a chance for a few Aussies to learn a bit more about the people they share the country with as well.

While at Gunbalanya we stayed at the old guesthouse over-looking a floodplain full of birds and a beautiful weathered chunk of escarpment rising up in the distance. Having some proper facilities also gave me a break, and I got a chance to get to know Bulk, and the rest of the support crew. Bulk was a really interesting bloke who'd come from the East Coast and he'd been around a bit, and was a very capable truck driver and a good laugh. Ben and the pommy couple were excep-tionally good fun as well, and of-course there was Jungle Jacky.

By now the entire Chinese film mob had totally fallin in love with Jungle Jacky; I think they would have been more than happy just to make a film totally about her.

She sure was a fine example of Aussie womanhood, a sort of combination between Elle McPherson, a Bryon Bay Hippy and the Bush Tucker Man, and probably another main con-tributing factor for all the harmony in the camp. I wouldn't be surprised if she pops up in some Shanghai Soap Opera in the future.

I mean if this group of twenty-five Chinese loved her, why wouldn't the other Billion back home?

After a very pleasant time at the Gunbalanya guest house the convoy moved off once more. 'Bulk' the skinny truck driver led the way as we rocked and rolled over some more fierce corrugations heading out on the Maningrida road. I suppose we went about three or four hours and crossed count-less crystal clear creeks that cut across the track. The Chinese couldn't believe how vast and untouched a lot of this area was, and the fact you could just lean out of your vehicle and drink the sweet water blew their minds a bit.

Every so often the convoy would stop, just to give the film crew an opportunity to film Jungle Jacky looking good next to her Four Wheel Drive.

We finally left the track and turned off onto a smaller track that wound its way up to a group of shacks on top of a hill called Namagadabu. This was to be our final camping spot and with the help of a few professional hunters that were using this spot as their base, the Chinese were going to get stuck right in to some pig hunting. As Lou Man explained, hunting is keeping alive ancient Chinese traditions and it's a proud part of their ancestor's way of life. So the next few days were spent mainly filming the pig hunting and stuff.

The pro hunters were great blokes, and they had a few good dogs with them as well, preferring to hunt the old fashion way, just stalking the animal and then the chase, followed by the wrestle, and finally stabbing it in the heart, bringing about a quick death. No mean feat with a feral pig.

So across the floodplains and through the scrub they went, feral pigs running for their lives followed by a pack of dogs, followed by the hunters trying to keep up to the dogs, followed by a Chinese film crew trying to keep up to the hunters trying to keep up to the dogs.

All galloping across the flat.

For those few days we camped at Namagadabu, pigs must have felt very nervous. Everyone got to stick one, I even think Little Fatty stuck one. Jungle Jacky tried to get me to go out but I was quite happy being the cook as I've killed plenty of animals in my day but not by choice, and it's something I like to leave to someone else. But in that country pigs have taken over a bit, and so eradicating them is a good thing for the environment, although the pigs would probably disagree.

One morning the strapping sensitive Ben walked past the fire in a trance. They'd taken him out pig hunting the night before and he got to stick one. He just wandered through the camp muttering 'Just flip em and stick em', 'They told me to just flip em and stick em'. I don't think it agreed with his

Author Phil O'Brien extends the hand of friendship.

sensitive nature very much, and he was in shock for most of the day.

One Chinese bloke got shown how to traditionally kill a File Snake the Aboriginal way. Normally the head of the snake is placed in your mouth and you bite down on its head to hold it in place, and at the same time jerk its body back the other way, this instantly kills the snake.

The Chinese bloke was so worked up he bit its head clean off. They were very enthusiastic.

By now, my traditional Aussie style campfire cooking was taking on a more oriental slant, thanks to the Chinese translator who was also acting as my cooking coach. Up till then my favourite herb had been salt, but now nothing left the campfire without being doused severely with Soy Sauce and infused with Garlic and Ginger.

I'd even progressed onto stir-fry, and she was a great help. We only nearly came to blows once and that was during a big rice boil up. She had her way of doing it and I had mine and there was a clash, but once I reminded her that I was the bloke actually cooking the stuff, she settled down a bit. I understood her concerns though, because telling a Chinese how to cook rice, is like telling an Eskimo how to make ice cubes, or an Italian how to make Pizza – they're always gunna fire up.

Namagadabu had its own magic; although the bush was a bit scrappy there and the scenery wasn't quite as impressive as the other spots, it boasted one remarkable and very rare landmark.

A phone box!

Right in the middle of nowhere was a payphone powered by a solar panel, and it was a Minor Success because it actually worked.

Alex Wu the radio presenter from Beijing couldn't believe his luck. So with a pocketful of coin he spoke live on Beijing

Calling Beijing

radio to millions of people across China, telling them about this great adventure.

For some reason it was all pretty emotional.

To me it was Arnhem Land opening up her heart, and I nearly shed a tear into a big drum of Chow Mein I was brewing up at the time.

That night I got the guitar out and we had a bit of a sing-a-long and I sang an old Eric Clapton song called 'Talk to me Baby', and as a bit of a tribute to Alex Wu I changed it to 'Talk to me Beijing'.

It seemed more appropriate.

A full moon came up over the hill while we were camped at Namagadabu, laden with passion it stirred the fires of romance a bit, and as the moon got higher and the flames grew stronger I looked across the smouldering coals of my campfire

Jungle Jacky [aka Jacqui Taylor] A great example of Australian womanhood.

to the beautiful Jungle Jacky - and dropped the weights on her.

I was hoping we could hit the swag together and go up in smoke. Unfortunately, the raging flames of this romantic heartfelt fire weren't ever destined to spread, and Jungle Jacky responded just like a CFS Unit would... she put them out.

It was a good trip but it wasn't that good.

The Chinese rolled some more film, stuck a few more pigs, and it was time to once again pack up, and this time unfortunately, head for home,

What a great ten days, made memorable by good people.

Bulk the skinny truck driver always good for a yarn, Little Fatty, Major Zi, Alex Wu, the pommy backpackers, hard swearing Lou-Man, the strapping but sensitive Ben, and not to mention the charismatic Jungle Jacky, it was a crazy bunch but for some reason it was all very comfortable being around them.

The Aboriginal hospitality as well was warm and generous, as only they can be.

We dropped the Chinese film mob off at a resort in Kakadu on our way back to Darwin, as they were using another support crew for that leg of their trip.

I was sad to see them go. Friendships were made and anyone that had anything to do with the Chinese found them very likable. It just goes to show you, and I've always thought this, it's not a good place that makes a good situation. Good people make a good situation.

I mean you could end up sitting under a mulga bush out in the Simpson Desert drinking beer at gearbox temperature, it wouldn't matter, if you're with a good mob, you'll have a good time where ever you are.

It's the people that make it.

They were a hardy lot, and it wasn't hard to work out why the Chinese were such an important part of our history and development as a country especially during the early pioneering stages.

I hope the TV series works out and I'm sure it will.

It was a real Minor Success to see people from very diverse cultures working and sharing experiences together.

As I said my goodbyes I felt inspired, but I also felt a little confused, I was thinking Hey - if different peoples can get on so well together...

Why can't the governments?

GET THE OXY

NORTHERN TERRITORY CATTLEMAN Ben Tapp hasn't always been a legend, he wasn't quite born one, and like everyone else when he was a young bloke he had to go through that 'Jackeroo' phase. A Jackeroo is like an apprentice stockman and usually gets lumbered with some of the shit jobs older blokes aren't real interested in any more.

One Christmas Ben and his mate had to stay behind and keep an eye on the family property, while everyone else went into town for a blow out. Apart from the two young lads there was just an old handyman type bloke that used to work there. Ben and his mate hadn't seen the old feller around for a few days, so they thought they'd better have a check, just to make sure something unforseen hadn't happened to him. Sure enough there he was, flat on his back choked out in his room, and he looked pretty well dead. There were a lot of empty beer and rum bottles lying around, and who knows what happened, a stroke or seizure or the like.

Anyways he didn't look real good.

Shit, what do we do now they thought, there's the old bloke, not moving, pale, and vomit caked all over his mouth and face.

'Well I'm not givin him mouth to mouth' Ben reckoned.

'No way, I'm just not doin it'.

Then his young mate thought for a while and he reckoned, 'I've heard you can give them sick people oxygen'.

'Oxy'... Ben reckoned. 'We got Oxy'.

So they raced down to the workshop and grabbed the Oxy bottle and dragged it up to this bloke's room, and they took the handpiece off and shoved the hose down his throat, and turned the tap on. He blew up like a balloon and his eyes shot open. Ben and his mate just kept working the tap pumping him up, pumping him up, thinking they were doing a great job. The bloke's eyes getting wider. Then they alerted the Flying Doctor and he got there within an hour or so, and took the old feller straight to intensive care up in Darwin.

A few days later Ben rang the hospital to see if the old bloke pulled through...

'Yeah he made it' the Doctor reckoned, 'but all his throat's burnt out'!

It was a Minor Success for a lot of people Ben never pursued a career in First Aid, and he stuck to cattle.

WATERMELON PICKING

WATERMELON PICKING is one reason why young people should stay at school and try and successfully complete year 12. It's one reason why young people should go to Uni, or join the army, become a Priest, or a career criminal, or an I.T expert, it doesn't matter. What ever you do don't ever get that broke, or down and out, that you have to pick watermelons to survive. Believe me - it ain't pretty.

The truck picked us up while it was still dark. In the centre of town we gathered.

A collection of losers.

Why were we there? Good question. Obviously everyone's lives weren't going as well as they would have liked.For a few like me there weren't many actual options, I'd travelled a fair way to start a new job, but it had fallen straight through.

Being an eternal optimist doesn't always prepare you for these types of situations. You never actually think things aren't gunna work out, you live in hope, so you don't worry about having enough to back you up just in case. Then all your plans turn to shit, because the bloke you're meant to be working for turns out to be a wanker.

Looking around at the rest of the group climbing on to the back of the truck, I'd say I wasn't the only one who hadn't had a minor success for a while.

I recognised one bloke, I'm sure he used to be the wildlife ranger around here a few years back, must have fallen on hard times, and those backpackers - the girl with the dreadlocks smelt like an old 'Polecat', and why was that middle aged lady with the two black eyes here, and that miserable looking pensioner couple? Maybe it was obvious.

Twenty people climbing onto the back of a truck.

Twenty people desperately needing a few bucks.

Twenty people heading off to pick watermelons.

Twenty people down on their luck.

Fuck.

The mood on the back of the truck as we headed out of town couldn't really be described as festive. No-one was congratulating anyone else on securing such a great bit of employment, no-one was patting anyone else on the back and celebrating the fact we were about to get a whopping nine dollars an hour, and it was only going to be about 50 degrees Celsius that day.

We looked like a mob of slaves that had just been rounded up. No-one spoke, we just stared into each other's sunken eyes. About thirty kilometres later we're at the farm, and some bloke's barking commands at us.

'INTO THE FIELDS!' - 'INTO THE FIELDS!'

Just like a rugby drill, we're tossing watermelons from ground level up and across from person to person till its journey ended with the bloke stacking them in the crate on the back of the tractor. Go Go Go, faster...faster!

We're fanning out and we're going hard, trying to keep up

with the bloke in the tractor. After a few hours we were all bent over like crabs, trying to keep up, no time to straighten up, just throw those melons.

It was stinking hot and the only time anyone got a drink was when someone dropped a melon and it broke open, people were just grabbing the red fleshy part and squashing it and getting a few drips out of it, desperately wetting their lips.

Some of the group walked off and decided to take their chances with the thirty kilometre hike back to town. They'd rather do a 'Burke and Wills'.

Come lunch time what was left of the team flaked it in this old tin shed and the boss bloke rolled a watermelon in, and threw us a pocket knife.

There was about eight of us left at that stage, not counting the old pensioner couple who were still lying out in the field, I think they were dead.

After lunch we worked straight through till sunset, and on the truck heading back to town I counted six people.

Next morning I turned up again and there were about twenty people waiting to meet the truck. I didn't recognise any of them; it was a completely new mob.

I knew it would be, I knew no one would put themselves through that again, except me, I just wanted to prove I came from good stock. But that was my last day, then I quit as well.

So the moral of this story is simple, next time you're at a fruit and veg shop or local supermarket and you're there checking out the melons... please, please quietly gather the people near you together, and hold hands, light a few candles, and have a minutes silence, and show some respect... For the poor bastards that picked them.

THE V8 SUPERCARS

LAST TIME SOMEONE SAID 'It's an emergency can you help me out' was Steve the Mackerel fisherman, and that little foray on the high seas nearly ended up with me being torn apart by sharks. I'd come as close as I ever wanted to get to becoming shark shit.

So I vowed to put a bit more thought into the things I get involved in.

But even as responsible as that line of thinking is, when a mate asks you for a hand in a crisis it's very hard to do anything but get involved.

The V8 Supercars were in town preparing to battle it out at Hidden Valley Raceway.

Holden and Ford - petrol-guzzling gladiators.

It was gunna be a struggle for supremacy down in the valley of the giants. The Northern Territory was all fired up as usual with the annual hugely popular racing car event.

Forty thousand hardened race fans were expected to make the trip to Hidden Valley for the weekend, to cheer on their heroes.

Russel Ingall – The Enforcer.

The Kelly Brothers – Rough and Ready
Skaifey – The Magician.
Craig Lowndes – The Gentleman.

All the big guns were in town to put pedal to the metal and forty thousand race fans were preparing to wildly follow every lap, right down to the last burnout.

Car racing was never my scene; I preferred the quiet solitude of a campfire out bush with just a guitar for company. I'd never been to a car race, and I knew nothing about car racing. I wasn't interested in motor sports of any kind. Little kids and family pets probably knew more than I did about car racing, and it didn't worry me in the least. It was never gunna be a problem.

Then one day that all changed.

A friend called Simon Manzies who had his own TV production company got in touch with me. He had a real situation on his hands. He had the contract to film stuff at the V8's, mainly interviews with the crowd and racing car drivers, anything to do with the race. It was to be shown on these huge screens positioned around the raceway, basically to keep everyone entertained in-between events.

'Big problem', he reckoned.

'The girl that normally would be presenter and do all the interviewing and stuff has dropped out at the last minute really leaving me in the poo'.

'Was there a chance I'd be interested'?

Simon was definitely up against it, time was running out, but he had a feeling I could really make a go of it.

How Simon came to that conclusion I'll never really know.

I had been in one of those T.V ads he made about pool safety a while back, but all I had to do was make out I was cooking a barbeque, and tell this bunch of kids to shut the gate. Either he saw some real talent there, or else he was even more desperate than he made out.

Probably the latter.

Anyway, I think he had more confidence in me than what I had in myself. Of all the 200 plus jobs I've had in my life there's been nothing like this. Roving reporter, oh shit? Then a vision of my bank balance flashed before my eyes, things were getting lean. Simon was offering pretty good money so as with Steve the Mackerel Fisherman, I threw myself in the deep end.

This time it wasn't sharks that were going to be the threat, it will be forty thousand screaming revved up race fans, and I don't know what's wilder?

Simon gave me a little pocket handbook on V8 Supercars. All the information I needed, driver's names and their backgrounds, and all about the track. It was great but the race was the next day.

It was like - a bloke needs a heart transplant operation and someone just gives you a book about hearts and says 'O.K. just whack one into him'!

I mean it's a big ask.

That evening I think I was about as nervous as I've ever been in my life. I wished I were back in Arnhem Land farming Crocodiles, because that was way less stressful than what I'd just got myself into. Then I drifted back to when I was a Jackeroo riding an out of control bolting horse, heading straight for a cliff. I even think that was less nerve racking.

Mackerel fishing with Steve was close however, bobbing around huge seas in a little dinghy with great packs of sharks following you around. That was terrifying.

But I think the V8's had the edge on that one as well.

With a sleepless night under my belt I headed down to Hidden Valley Raceway, the valley of the giants. Not only would Holden and Ford be battling it out, but so would Phil O'Brien. All I could remember from the handbook Simon gave me was that Hidden Valley had a really long 'Straight'.

My depth of knowledge on car racing was now complete; I could fit it all on the back of a postage stamp.

Now I know what a bullock feels like as it's heading down to the meatworks.

Simon was there to meet me in the car park shortly after sunrise. Even at this early hour people were rolling in by the droves. Buses one after the other threading their way into the raceway. Crowds of people with their flags and scarves and T-Shirts all displaying either Holden or Ford logos. It was like I'd come to a battleground, with two tribes getting ready to fight it out. There was colour and movement everywhere. The sound coming from the pits was already deafening, as the V8's like roosters, were singing in the new day.

The more the mighty V8's barked and roared the bigger the smiles on the fanatical fans' faces, and the livelier they stepped as they headed for their positions around the track.

Simon had a special media access pass, this allowed him to drive his car through the outer part of the arena down past the pit area to a small bunker, and he was using this as his headquarters for the big weekend.

As we weaved slowly down the access road through the crowd, people started pressing their faces up against the car window trying to look in.

Obviously they thought it must have been someone famous. But it wasn't, it was just me, and I was staring back... in shock. My arse was already starting to smoulder.

We eventually made it down to Simons bunker headquarters just past what they call 'Pit Lane'.

Pit Lane was where most of the noise was coming from, and it was all go. Blokes in brightly coloured overalls were running everywhere, cars revving frantically, officials with their orange vests and walkie talkies bolting around looking very official. Fire marshals suited up in their space suits waiting for a fire to start, so they could put it out, and some eye catching, rip snorting, female talent.

Stunning looking women, with skimpy little outfits, that had more hanging out than what was being held in, were scattered in around the action. Most of the V8 teams had a few of these promotional girls around to advertise various sponsor's products, and they were pretty tidy.

Blokes were flocking around them getting their photo taken and it was smiles all around, and also the odd tongue hangin out.

Hidden Valley was starting to crank right up.

From what I could gather, on this particular weekend nothing else mattered. Tsunamis, World War Three, Global Warming, Haley's Comet... it didn't matter. All that mattered to the thousands of fans was Holdens and Fords, and the only place to be on Earth this weekend was Hidden Valley.

I asked Simon if he had anymore books on car racing, and he casually reckoned don't worry I wont need them. All you gotta do he said was go up to people and say 'Holden or Ford'? and the rest will fall into place, trust me.

I wished I had his confidence.

I met the cameraman and got a few last minute tips on how to use the microphone, and then it was get out there and go for it. Phil O'Brien the official presenter, car-racing guru, the full bottle.

'Trust me', Simon kept saying.

The cameraman led the way as we pushed up Pit Lane.

I thought seriously about giving the microphone to the cameraman and running off. The only thing that kept me there was the fact I'd given Simon me word.

First interview, I took a deep breath and went up to this Bikie looking bloke pointed the microphone at him and like Simon reckoned, I just said 'Holden or Ford'?

Well, bugger me, the guy's eyes lit up and he went off, waving his great fists around and screaming and yelling something about Ford rules, and Holden sucks eggs. I stood there agreeing with everything he said as the camera rolled. It was easy.

Next interview I just walked up to this peaceful looking family and said 'Holden or Ford'?

The whole family went completely wild; Granny, Mum, Dad, the kids, all waving their flags and chanting 'Hol-dens', 'Hol-dens', and then another bunch of Holden fanatics came running over and waved more flags with Holden splashed across them. I just nodded and went along with whatever they screamed at me.

Hey, this jobs not too bad I'm thinkin.

After about an hour of doing this I was starting to get a bit excited as well. The V8 fever was starting to grab me, I mean you couldn't help but get swept away in it along with everyone else. Simon was right. He knew I didn't know Jack shit about car racing, but he knew I'm the type of bloke that gets excited really easy.

So the informative interviews continued, I don't think I'll ever get a job on '60 Minutes' but I tell you what, I was getting good at asking who was gunna win - 'Holden or Ford'?

After the fume filled chaos of Pit Lane, me and the cameraman headed into Merchandise Alley where all the racing teams sell their T-Shirts and Caps etc. Merchandise Alley was filling up with race fans stocking up on their hero's gear, and there was quite a few promotional girls getting around as well. I chalked up a few more interviews. By now the words Holden or Ford was just rolling off the tongue. Smooth as silk.

Through the crowd we went, interview after interview, people going crazy with devotion for either Holden or Ford, and me agreeing with everything because I didn't know any better. Then two steaming hot promotional girls caught my eye, they were promoting Valvaline Engine Oil. These two girls weren't just good looking, they were smokin.

So I thought I better interview them as well.

I mean, if you're gunna be a professional interviewer you've got to interview a complete cross section of the crowd. If that means a few stunners, well, hey, it's a dirty job but someone's got to do it.

I introduced myself and they seemed all keen for a chat to the camera so I got in the middle between them with my microphone and we cuddled up a bit, then the camera started rolling. Before I had a chance to deliver me standard Holden or Ford line, one of them looked at me all suggestively and then looked at the camera and reckoned, 'I could dip my stick anytime!'... And she said it with a fair bit of conviction as well.

I wasn't ready for that one.

There I am, just standing there frozen, my hand holding the microphone started shaking wildly. The camera's rolling, I'd forgotten what to say, and I couldn't help but stare at her breasts...and that was about as in-depth as that interview got.

Where does Simon find em, the cameraman was probably thinking?

I sure did meet some fantastic people at the V8's. It seemed to me like the race fans even though they followed either Holden or Ford fanatically, there was no animosity between them. They were comrades sharing the one cause, and that was the race itself. The action, the noise, the fumes, the burnt rubber, and the revelry.

The V8 crowd was a real fraternity, and in their own way they shared the love. I never saw any trouble at all as I wandered around.

Apart from the strong sense of unity with the race fans, the other really refreshing thing about the V8's was the disregard of any modern day political correctness. In a world that's getting wound up tighter than a fishes arse, its hard to know what to say or how to act anymore, without offending someone, or some highly strung minority group.

But not at the V8's.

Men could be men and women could be women.

By this I mean a bloke could swill on a few beers, get off on the primeval pleasure of watching cars go fast, yell, scream, pass wind, and let a good lookin woman know she's lookin good. Harmless adoration.

Women could do the same, and it was totally acceptable behaviour for the V8 family. It was raw and honest, without any stigmas being attached, and by mid morning I was converted.

They were my type of people.

Me and the cameraman were going pretty good notching up quite a few more interviews on the big screens, and my tongue tied state of shock with the Valvaline Girls was pretty well forgotten, as we slid through the crowd. Simon rang the cameraman on his mobile; 'All the drivers are hanging around Pit Lane because a race is due to start, get back there and interview a driver' he reckoned. So back to noisy Pit Lane we trotted.

What do you say to a racecar driver when you don't know

anything about car racing?

The drivers were elite athletes in their own right, and totally worshipped by the fans. So whatever you say to them it had to be reasonably intelligent. You couldn't just pull out the old Holden and Ford what do you reckon?

That would have been an insult.

The first driver we tracked down was Mark Skaife, or Skaifey as he is affectionately known to his legion of supporters. Skaifey was a big name and enjoys a high profile in the sport. We could see him in his pit area getting ready and the cameraman started to panic a bit because the race would start soon and he didn't want to miss a scoop with Skaifey.

So he told me in no uncertain terms to 'Friggen get in there'!

As I approached Skaifey he turned and waved his hand in a gesture that translated, basically meant 'Piss off'. So I turned to go out, and the cameraman's telling me to 'Friggen get back in there', and so I turn to go back and there's Skaifey gesturing me to 'Piss off' again.

Oh this is great I'm thinkin'.

If you've ever tried to hold two magnets together you soon realize you can't do it because there's this freaky zone in-between them that wont let them connect. Well, that's the zone I felt like I was in.

The stalemate repeated itself a few more times and then Skaifey finally took pity on me and came up and said 'O.K. Lets go'. So the camera rolled and I dug deep into my depth of knowledge and released everything I knew about car racing in one big whopping question...

'Mark what do you think about the long straight here at Hidden Valley'?

'Tremendous', he reckoned, then he put his helmet on and

took off. The interview wasn't what you'd call riveting, but I survived.

With that one under me belt we headed back to Simon's bunker for a break. The first race wasn't far off and all the red-hot promotional girls had formed up just near the bunker getting ready to parade out onto the track in a bit of a fanfare. Then their job was to stand there looking good and hold an umbrella over each individual racecar driver, and give him a bit of shade, as the officials go through the formalities of the start.

It was really an exciting and colourful spectacle, but in some circles of society I suppose they'd view women holding umbrellas above men's heads as discrimination, degrading, and an attack on women's rights. Why not have a bloke? they'd reckon, or just a beach umbrella tied to a Besser Block. Why does it have to be a scantily clad hot looking babe?

Well, I think the answer to that is quite obvious.

In the sun everyone knows the best thing to keep the sun off is a beautiful young girl with an umbrella. Everyone knows that. Society knows that. Skin cancer specialists know that. Women's rights movements have known that for years.

The thing is outside the V8's, it's just hard gettin girls to do it. But at the V8's political correctness stops at the gates like I said, and if the girls feel good lookin good, and the crowd feels good lookin at them look good... then it's all good.

This is what makes the V8's unique; it's an event that still supports the old fashioned Aussie values.

After another coffee in the bunker, the V8's exploded in a mighty roar as the first race ignited. Off they went screaming around the track. The noise was deafening as the sleek machines jostled and negotiated the Hidden Valley circuit with anger and precision.

Simon reckoned he'd organised something really special for when the race finishes. Up at Merchandise Alley there was the strongest man in the world doing power-lifting exhibitions. He was lifting big V8 engine blocks and other incredibly heavy objects that normally would take a crane to lift. Simon had tee-ed up a wrestling match between him and me.

'The crowd will love it'! He light heartedly hooted away.

As Simon continued, one word reverberated around in my head, and it started with a capital F and ended in c-k.

This whole set up wasn't sounding real pretty, I'm thinkin.

I was going to cop a pizzling all in the name of entertainment. But there was no swaying Simon; this was going to be a cracker!

The race finally came to a thunderous climax, and the cheering and heavy revving faded off, and a warm contented lull came over Hidden Valley.

It was like the crowd had just had sex and was now relaxing with a cigarette, savouring the moment. This was my cue to go and get bashed by the strongest man in the world.

Up Merchandise Alley I plodded and there he was, rough and chunky, a man mountain. His legs were like River Red Gums, forearms like giant pistons, and his neck was like a Mallee stump, and balanced on top of it was a shiny shaved wild lookin head.

He was walking around with a V8 engine block tucked under his arm as if it were a carton of beer, and he was coming back from the bottle shop. The strong man put it down and came over; he'd been expecting the cameraman and me.

I bloody well hoped Simon had worker's compensation insurance, because I think I'll probably be putting in a claim in about five minutes, I thought to myself.

Over he came and a smile broke out on his huge dial and he had a bit of a laugh, and we shook hands and introduced ourselves. He was actually a really nice bloke and so I felt a bit better about the whole thing. He's just a gentle giant I'm thinkin. I doubt whether he's very aggressive at all.

He's just too nice a bloke.

Then the camera rolled and the top bloke gentle giant picked me up and swung me around his head half a dozen times like a wet towel, and then speared me into the concrete.

'Oh yeah'! 'Wow wee'! The crowd loved it, they thought it was great. Simon was right again. Tremendous family entertainment. The strongman went back to doing his power lifting, and I staggered off.

Nothing like a quiet day at the races.

After the cameraman stopped pissing himself laughing he was keen to get some more interviews. I gathered myself up and banged down a feed of chicken and chips and was ready to press on. That was going to be a dreadfully hard act to follow, I was thinkin.

We headed back down towards Pit Lane, me head still spinning a little.

Out of the blue the cameraman pulled me up next to a stack of racing car tyres and told me to talk about the tyres. Before I had time to tell him I didn't know anything at all about racing car tyres, he started rolling the camera. This was gunna be tough.

There I was, I'd survived interviewing the frenzied crowd, I'd survived interviewing the big gun driver Skaifey, I'd survived the Valvaline Girls, and I'd survived being thrown around by the world's strongest man, and now it looked like my luck had finally run out.

The camera was rolling and my career as an interviewer at

the V8's hung precariously in the balance. I had to think quickly or else I was guuna look pretty stupid. I had no choice; I had to make something up.

This was going to be one of the best exhibitions of Bullshitting, ever Bullshitted, in the history of Bull-Shit.

The origins of these tyres, I said, could be dated back about 1,000 years to medieval England. This is where they used to perform the 'Smouldering the Shetland' ceremony.

All the young lads of the day used to meet at the local tavern on a Saturday night and have a few wines. Then they'd all get in their little carts which were drawn by a Shetland Pony, and head off to this cobble stoned area on the edge of town, and this is where they'd perform the 'Smouldering the Shetland' ceremony.

One bloke would hold the Shetland pony, and the others would poke him in the guts with a stick and hit him and stuff till the Shetland pony got really agitated, and it started to freak out. The Shetland Pony just wanted to go, so all of a sudden they'd let it loose, and on the cobble stones the Shetland would be trying to gallop off, but it couldn't get any traction on the cobble stones, and its little hooves would be goin that fast they'd start smokin up, trying to get traction on the cobble stones.

This is what they called 'Smouldering the Shetland'.

But sometimes they'd smoke up so much trying to get traction that they'd burn off the hoof back to the butt. This was no good because the Law Enforcement officers at the time used to run them off the road, 'Not enough tread on that Shetland Pony' they'd reckon. So over time the lads worked out they had to transform smokin them up at the front of the cart, to the rear.

So after a few more wines back at the tavern they put their

heads together, and they went out and invented rubber, solely for the purpose of smokin them up, and doing decent burnouts, and you heard it first right here... at Hidden Valley!

Well, that was it.

The cameraman was stunned.

The crowd was stunned, and I'd even stunned myself.

It was a Minor Success because the story was so way out, it was believable, and I got away with it.

I even heard people saying...

'Wow'! - 'This new bloke really knows his stuff'!

SYDNEY OR BUST

I'D WRITTEN ME FIRST BOOK '101 Adventures that have got me Absolutely Nowhere' volume one, and it had done really well, which surprised a lot of people - including me.

So I followed it up with the aptly titled 101 Adventures... volume two.

All up it had been yet another great experience writing down all me yarns but although I'd sold a fair few copies and I suppose you could say it was a success, financially I was once again on the bones of my arse. There are quite a lot of costs when it comes to printing and distributing your own books, and any profit I made was usually spent on the pursuit of happiness and a good time. I was living for the moment as usual without any real plan for the future. Nothing new.

Basically I'd sold all me stock of books and had nothing to show for it.

Life's full of ups and downs and I've never really questioned anything that's been thrown at me. I just try and stay positive and optimistic and never stop having a crack. It's a shame I can't handle my finances a bit better, but each day is a new day and with it brings new opportunities I always say. Somehow the ABC had got wind of my books and thought there was some potential there, and so they rang me up. The conversation went something like this...

'We really like your stories, but unfortunately they're as rough as guts', they reckoned. 'If you're interested we'd like to publish your stories but with a bit of editing and a more professional approach', they also reckoned.

I couldn't believe it, what an opportunity, I was thinkin.

So I got straight to the point and asked them what this all equated to as far as the 'hoot' went.

'Well Mr O'Brien the 'hoot' as you so delicately put it would see you getting a five thousand dollar advance', the voice on the other end of the line retorted.

'Five bloody what'! I replied with a fair bit of gusto.

In my mind I was already starting to spend it.

'Excuse me Mr O'Brien' replied the well-educated voice from an ABC office somewhere in Sydney.

'Yeah sounds great, what do we do now'? I asked.

'Well, we'll do up the contract and get it out to you in about ten days, and then we'll go from there', the long distance voice echoed.

We'll go from there alright, just wait till I get my hands on that five thousand, we'll go from there alright!

It looked like a timely bit of luck had come my way maybe even a potential Major Success, so I celebrated by putting a Slim Dusty cassette in the player and pumped down a six-pack. It was all good, the ABC was taking me seriously and when they said me stories were as rough as guts I somehow took that as a compliment. I swelled with pride as I started on me second six pack, and as Slim Dusty's country rhythms pounded and the Victoria Bitter flowed freely through my veins, I got one of the greatest ideas I'd ever conjured up in my whole life.

Why wait for the contract to be sent to Darwin?

I'd fly down to Sydney and meet them face to face, then sign the deal and get me wad of cash, and then hit Sydney with it. It all made perfectly good business sense. I'd never been to Sydney, I'd never seen the Opera House or the Harbour Bridge, this was a golden opportunity for the trip of a lifetime!

One week later...

The Qantas jet bucked and shook as we hit some turbulence rising up from the Blue Mountains, then all was calm again as we sailed through the clouds blanketing the outer suburbs of Sydney. Out across the blue sparkling ocean, then a big right-hander and in we went -'cabin crew prepare for landing'.

Everyone clawing at their armrests with anxiety, but still trying to make out they're not scared of flying. Then touch-down, we made it – 'cabin crew disarm doors' went the deep voice over the loud speaker.

We can all stop shitting bricks now I'm thinkin. Not being one for flying, but it beats driving; it probably would have taken me eighteen months to drive from Darwin to Sydney the way I travel.

Besides, I had money to spend and there was no time to waste.

So in the footsteps of Captain James Cook back in seventeen seventy something, I stepped out of the departure lounge, curious to see what promises this new land would bring.

Firstly I couldn't believe the size of the airport, a bloke needed a cut lunch and a water bag just to find his way out. But not only that, someone had built a railway station underneath it! Down I went riding an escalator that seemed to be going way too fast. Sydney had the fastest escalators I'd ever ridden; everyone's hair was flying back in the breeze as we sped down heading for the underground railway station. I'm thinkin, what happens when you get to the bottom?

I was all set to just throw me suitcase and go into a commando roll.

Then I saw the bloke in front of me sort of crow hop. He looked like he was a veteran of quite a few escalator trips, so I followed his style and just tried to crow hop off as well, and went arse up.

No one stopped - they just walked over me.

In Darwin if you fell over like that someone would probably lie down next to you roll a smoke and have a yarn. But Sydney was an up-tempo city, and it was all go and obviously only the strong survived.

How embarrassing I was thinking, as I trotted off trying to keep up with the crowd. Then we all jammed ourselves onto a train heading for 'Circular Quay'. The train roared off like a shower of shit and it only took maybe fifteen minutes and there we were at Circular Quay, right in the middle of Sydney.

It really was a sight; the harbour with its ferries coming and going with their trails of foamy white-water, the Opera House was right there, and the Harbour Bridge dominated the panorama impressively.

For modern day Australia this was the 'dreaming place', this is where it all started. I never thought that being in the middle of a huge city could move me so much, but I suppose I'd grown up with icons like the Opera House and the Bridge, and now finally I was seeing them in real life, and it definitely set me back in me tracks a bit.

So there I was just absorbing the whole emotional moment, not quite sobbing but to the Sydney mob racing around it probably looked like I was having a 'breakdown' or a 'stroke' or something, but anyway it wasn't enough to make anyone stop. Once again in Darwin someone probably would have rushed up and invited you to a barbeque at their place.

But this was Sydney, there was no time for sensitive emotional moments, there was no time to look for a friend, there were contracts to sign and a cheque to smash. It was time for a man to walk tall.

Only problem was that it was a Sunday and I couldn't do the business till Monday. Probably time to settle down a bit and drop the suitcase off, and go do some sight seeing, I was thinkin.

I boarded what appeared to be a normal looking taxi, but two minutes into the trip I realised this was the taxi from hell. He cut off busses, he cut off cars, and you name it, he cut it off. I wondered if they were all like this?

This guy was rogue, and he was at war with every living thing that used the road. He was scaring the shit out of me as he reefed the wheel from left to right, weaving in and out of the busy traffic. Even when he pulled up to let me out he stopped in a bus stop... with a bus fair up his arse. The people that got off the bus gave him the fingers, and it was all pretty heated, but it didn't seem to worry him, he just sped off.

Next time I think I'll just use the foot falcon and walk I told myself, as I booked into my accommodation.

The Backpackers I was staying at would have been great if you were into early architecture, and I wondered how many convicts died putting this one together. Anyway it was cheap and I didn't have a lot of money on me, but that would change as soon as I signed the big contract with the ABC.

There was no doubt in my mind the whole deal with the ABC would just be a smooth transition. That is, the $5000 would slide smoothly from their hand into mine, then smoothly into my pocket.

Then it was gunna be 'Oh... Baby Baby'

Like I said - a smooth transition.

I decided to hit the streets in search of something to eat and calm down a bit, there were so many good times up ahead it wasn't funny. The excitement of being in Sydney, and just the thought of having five thousand big ones exploding out of my pocket was giving me a big appetite.

I noticed as I was walking around there were a lot of Chinese people, virtually everyone and every shop owner was Chinese, which got me wondering. Then I was intercepted by a great aroma wafting out of one little place, so I headed in and was greeted by this Chinese woman, and I said 'I'm just lookin for a feed', she stared at me for a while, smiled, and said 'we no sell CD's'.

I think I was her first contact with European people.

So I pointed to a picture of a duck up on the wall and she got the message. I tell you what she couldn't speak much English, but she could cook a mean duck. Duck must have been popular because they were hanging everywhere, all the little shops had them dangling all over the joint.

Sydney had a real Beijing feel about it I thought to myself as I demolished the duck. Must be a sister city... then I saw the welcome to Chinatown sign.

It was the Chinatown area of the city.

Oh well... that cleared things up a bit.

The afternoon went by as I walked around and it was so interesting being in a different environment, and as I strolled through the streets of Sydney it was absolutely fascinating. Old buildings dating back, next to modern office blocks rising up, beautiful harbour views, and well dressed people moving briskly in and out the place.

The 'Monorail' roared overhead and I'm thinkin 'when did they invent that'?

I felt like a little kid walking around wide-eyed and naive.

After a while I ended up down at the Circular Quay area again and so I wandered innocently into a bar at a place they call 'The Rocks'. This Irish band was really pumping out some old fashioned Irish music, which inspired me to have a few quiet ones.

Last thing I remember was falling passionately in love with the girl playing the fiddle, but it was no good because by the time she noticed me staring and came over for a yarn, I was that drunk I couldn't speak. I woke up back at the Backpackers in Chinatown next day with no idea how I got there, who knows, maybe a blind bloke lent me his guide dog?

I was that crook there was no way I could face the ABC, so I rang them and postponed the meeting till the next day. I told them I had Gastro.

I didn't fire at all till well after lunch and I was pretty crook, but I thought I'd go out for a bit more of a look around. I felt shithouse because I blew the meeting, but I was in no state to talk turkey that's for sure, anyway the five big ones wouldn't be goin anywhere.

Not game to go near the Rocks area again, so this time I caught a bus out to a groovy looking suburb called Balmain. I had an old mate out there Geoff Morrison who ran his own graphic arts business called 'Bodgie Graphics' but there was nothing bodgie about Geoff's graphics. He was a gun, and had been a great help in pulling my first two books together ready for the printer, and with out his assistance I don't think it would have happened.

After a good catch up with Geoff at his rustic little Balmain cottage, I thought I'd have a wander.

Balmain was a happening little spot with great views of the harbour and heaps of cool little shops. So I thought I'd take the opportunity to buy a pair of new jeans for the big upcoming meeting. It was extravagant, but I'd soon be cashed up, thanks to the ABC.

Walking into this menswear place this bloke minces up to me with this tape measure draped around his neck. I couldn't work out if he was metro, hetro, or retro.

'Mmmmm... can I help you' he asks, and then puts one end of the tape measure into his mouth and started sucking it suggestively. I asked him if he had any cheap jeans?

'We sure have, our prices start from two hundred and twenty dollars', he reckoned, very excitably in a high pitched squeal. Where I come from you can buy a car for that I told him, and then I asked him where the nearest K-Mart was. His face dropped, and in a much deeper voice he said. 'Try Bondi Junction'.

A few bus trips later I found Bondi Junction and went into this gigantic shopping complex and then up an escalator, leapt off, and run fair into another really good old mate, Ray Drummond from Darwin. Ray had moved to Sydney a few years ago with this Air Hostess he'd tied up with. Well hows that! In a city of millions of people.

We both agreed this chance meeting had made us both a bit thirsty.

Next day I was even more crook than the day before,

I'd forgot Ray could push through liquid like a Pilot Whale, and the session went way into the night.

I rang the ABC and asked them if I could postpone the meeting to the next day. Couldn't shake the Gastro I told them. I felt like shit on a stick till well into the arvo, and just managed to walk out into Chinatown and eat a duck. Then I slowly picked up a bit.

That night I laid low, I had no choice anyway, I was nearly broke, and so I just tried to focus on my meeting with the ABC. A lot of writers would give their left ball for a publishing deal with the ABC, and I was just realising what an opportunity it was. No need to worry about the contract though I'm thinking, because the ABC are totally Australian and they are there to promote Australians, so no way were they going to shaft an Aussie with a dodgy contract. They were solid as a rock so it basically was just a formality, go in sign up... and collect the cabbage.

Next morning I was up and at 'em pretty early.

After a coffee and a duck in Chinatown I located the big ABC building spot on time for the meeting.

The building was a real rabbit warren; there were studios and offices everywhere. I headed for the enquiry counter. The bloke at the counter was that posh he sounded like he was trying to talk with a mouth full of ball bearings, and I could just picture him tipping chardonnay on his corn flakes for breakfast. After a bit of a 'ho' and a 'hum' the old boy sent me in the right direction, and all the excitement was now coming to a crescendo.

This was it! Contract time.

Sign up, and collect... oh yeah.

Five thou'

Hubba! Hubba!

The office door slowly squeaked open, and I was welcomed in by a friendly sophisticated lady in her early thirties. She was quite charming as we sat opposite each other and discussed the Northern Territory and my writing, and how happy she was that we were entering into this literary collaboration. It was all very pleasant, then she produced the contract and I had a quick scan and as I thought, it all looked pretty straightforward. Well the bit I read anyway. Then I signed.

Patiently I waited a minute wondering if she was gunna hand over a $5,000 cheque, or just a wad of straight cash. I looked at her, then she looked at me, and then I stared back at her and she looked at me, and she says 'Is everything alright?'

I think I must have looked like one of those dogs that hang around the kitchen table when you're having a feed, and it just looks up all doe eyed and hopeful it might get something. I stared back at her anxious, waiting, and my mouth getting dry.

'Have you got a question Mr O'Brien'?

I spat out a mumbled version of the word 'add add va va va vance'.

'Oh the advance' she reckoned, 'That should be processed in about three or four or maybe five or six weeks, and then you'll get half, and the other half after the editing process is completed, some time down the track'.

I found that I gulped that hard on hearing the news that me Adams Apple felt like it was gunna fire out me arse like a cannon ball.

But... but, but there were no buts.

I'd got it wrong, you don't get it all in one go, and it takes a while to come through, and I was broke. I should have asked more questions when we talked on the phone in Darwin, but I didn't because the moment I heard the words five thousand, I started living in a fantasy world.

I told her my plight, but this was the deal.

She was nice about it, but the ABC cogs turn slowly she

'Where's my five thousand?'

said, and this is the process, and that was that. We shook hands then it was back to Chinatown.

I felt a little depressed so I ate another duck.

Bloody bureaucracy I'm thinkin, surely she could have just given me the money out of her own savings.

It was Sydney or bust all right... and I'd just busted.

Me plans were well and truly thrown to the shithouse.

The froff had just gone off the cappuccino.

What now? I couldn't afford to swan around Chinatown anymore eating ducks, that's for sure. I didn't even have enough money to fly back to Darwin. What did they expect me to do now, piss in the gutter and swim home? The shine was slowly coming off this Major Success, but no need to panic, no need to be reactionary, but I should have bit her for a few hundred till payday.

Next morning I got up and booked a ticket on the Greyhound bus to Adelaide, this move being all the budget could support. I was gunna rock up at me mum's place, flat broke as usual, and just try and scrounge me way back to Darwin from there.

Oh well, I hoped to get back to Sydney another time, it had been really interesting, but I felt I just scratched the surface, there was so much more to see and do. But like the old saying goes, 'No Mun No Fun'.

My bus wasn't due to pull out till two in the arvo so I decided to chuck another lap of the city in the foot falcon and kill a bit of time, and see a few more sights.

I was moping along up this lane and out of nowhere I hear 'Eh Phil', 'Phil', so I turned around and I'll be stuffed, its this bloke and his missus that I met a few years ago back up in the Northern Territory. They'd gone and turned an old church into a real 'with it' café and had a good little business going.

I couldn't believe it, such a big city and I keep running into people I know.

'Come in we'll shout you breakfast' they reckoned, 'and meet our friend Sigrid'. I looked at Sigrid and I couldn't believe it, their friend Sigrid was none other than famous

Australian actress Sigrid Thornton.

She smiled warmly and held her hand out, and as our eyes met we shook gently. At that precise moment I felt like there was no one else around. No one else mattered. The Sydney streets were empty and void of all life.

Time stood still.

Sydney could have burnt down, blown up, and sunk, for all I cared.

Sigrid asked me to sit down and she didn't have to ask twice. I just threw myself down like a bloke at a party playing musical chairs, and this was the last chair. This lady was a class act and quite beautiful, with lively eyes that reflected a caring inner beauty as well.

She was really interested in my little expedition to Sydney, and we chatted away and she had plenty of good yarns herself from her life in show business. We swore, we laughed and we yarned away like old mates; well anyway, that's how she made me feel. It was just nice being around her.

Time was flying by.

It was now pushing midday and I knew I really should make a move if I was gunna make the Greyhound bus. But I was hypnotised by Sigrid's charm.

One o'clock came and went, and I couldn't even remember if I'd eaten the bacon and eggs or not. Things were getting critical, if I was to make the bus.

Two o'clock came, time to get my priorities straight.

What bus? Did someone mention a bus?

Sigrid smiled and chatted away, very genuine, very Aussie, and very charming. The hours just slipped away as we sipped coffee and shared a beautiful arvo, and I wouldn't have missed it for all the ducks in Chinatown.

It culminated with her asking me if I'd like to go see this

play she was in later that night, and she said there'd be a free ticket waiting there for me.

She was a gem all right, and the dream afternoon finally came to an end, and she had to take off and get prepared.

Soon after the beautiful Sigrid left I floated back down to earth and also to reality and in a panic I raced to a phone box and got onto the Greyhound bus mob. I knew I had to do some smooth talking because my ticket was a non-refundable one, which meant if you blow it, stiff cheddar, you lose your money and no way could I afford that, and as much as I enjoyed Sydney, I didn't want to end up living on the streets there.

'I had Gastro that bad I would have blown the bowl straight out the side of the bus', I told the Greyhound lady.

'Thankyou for that Mr O'Brien', she said very sympathetically.

The old Gastro's a pretty handy one to use in these situations because it conjures up some really disturbing images. I've found it pretty foolproof.

'Do you think you can make it tomorrow afternoon?' she politely asked me.

'Should be right' I groaned as if I was in a bit of pain.

Anyway that was a minor success in all its minor successful glory, so with me bus trip all squared away I headed back to my digs in Chinatown to book in for one more night. Then, with me last few bucks I bought a loaf of bread and a block of cheese for the bus trip to Adelaide.

I was now pretty well penniless but it didn't seem to worry me as I headed across town in search of the theatre Sigrid was performing in.

I couldn't remember actually ever being to many big plays before so I was pretty keen as I strode it out along the sidewalk.

I wondered what sort of play she was in. Maybe some stuffy old bullshit like 'Macbeth' or something, but who cares, she's in it and I'm going for free.

After a fairly lengthy walk I finally zero-ed in on the theatre. It was all pretty lavish with most of the people milling around dressed up to the nines. I turned a few heads as I marched in through the foyer and up to the ticket desk. I'm sure everyone thought I was in there just to try and bludge a cigarette.

'Are you right' the bloke in the penguin suite behind the counter asked me.

'Sigrid Thornton left me a ticket', I politely told him.

His head snapped around and his eyes nearly popped out of their sockets as he looked me up and down, and so I followed up with a 'Fair Dinkum'.

Sure enough, there it was, a free ticket.

I don't know who was more surprised... him or me.

It wasn't just your average free ticket either, it was front and centre, probably the best seat in the house. So off I went giving it a bit of the old swagger as I located my spot. Reclining back in the plush seat with the scent of expensive perfume and freshly dry-cleaned suits filling the air, I just couldn't believe it.

This was culture at its best.

The lights dimmed and out she came.

Sigrid Thornton - me mate.

What was she gunna say? What was this thing gunna be about? Shakespeare maybe? Opera? I had no idea. Maybe she was gunna break out singing 'Old Man River'. Hopefully it's not too boring. I moved on to the edge of my softly padded chair.

She said a few sentences with grace and style, walked up and down the stage a bit, and then took all her clothes off.

Now, I'm not sure about the rest of the theatre, but I know

me and about six blokes on my row needed CPR. There was nothing old fashioned about this play.

I had no idea I was gunna get to see so much of her in one day. Sigrid smouldered and sizzled her way through a brilliant performance. She really is one of Australia's premier actresses. The play was called the 'Blue Room' and it was basically about infidelity, which called for quite a lot of steamy scenarios. There also was a bloke in the play as well, but I never took much notice of him

It was a wonderful night and as I hoofed it back to China-town me top lip was still curled back just thinking about it.

I never saw Sigrid again, but why would I, we live in two completely different worlds, but I'll never forget what a down to earth pleasant person she was, and maybe a little sexy as well, but not only that, she actually had the decency to invite me to a play where she gets naked in.

I mean that really is 'true blue' in my books.

Next day as I boarded the Greyhound bus with me ten cheese sandwiches, I had a quick reflection on the time in Sydney. I'd come expecting the big wad from the ABC and I suppose the Major Success got watered down a bit, but it just goes to show you money isn't the only thing that brings happiness. Every day is a new day and with it brings a whole heap of new opportunities, and just maybe a Minor Success or two.

Sigrid sure proved that,

The funny thing is... on that trip to Adelaide I did feel like I had a bit of a crook guts coming on, maybe even some real genuine Gastro. But once again I was blessed with yet another Minor Success, because a few cheese sandwiches soon bunged that problem up.

IT'S AUSTRALIAN

I SUPPOSE IN THIS modern day and age we live in, we can sometimes lose track of who we are as a culture and a country. It's easy to get swept away with our cappuccinos, our Yiros's, our stir fry's, and all the other metro sexual, cross cultural, suburbanised influences that have now become the norm. But don't get me wrong, I think it's great we have all these different foods and customs and multicultural interactions as part of our modern day make up. I mean, when I was a kid a feed of fish and chips was about as exotic as it got. Things have really moved along, and this is a completely new age we live in. But it can be easy to forget just what it means to be an Australian, and what culture is all about.

Now, literary critics and a few women around the place both seem to have come to the conclusion that they reckon I'm slightly 'lacking' in culture, and after a few beers I also lack decorum. I'm not sure exactly what decorum means; I always thought it was a powder you use for 'chafe'. But the part about lacking in culture cuts pretty deep.

I mean, what's a bloke gotta do? You know, I was dining 'al fresco' before Alan Fresco even invented it? I can resoak me tea bags with the best of them, and I don't always drink red wine straight out the bottle.

Actually I'm a firm believer Holden's should still be producing 1966 HR Utes to satisfy the needs of the common man. So don't talk to me about culture. If I died tomorrow and they bottled my blood, there'd be 8 pints of pure culture... under corkage.

But OK, anyone can say that, anyone can blow their own horn. The proof's in the pudding. You have to produce the goods. This is why I decided to go off on a bit of a tangent.

I wanted to capture some real Australia for prosperity, just in case something happened to it. In years to come, who knows - maybe New Zealand will invade.

For safety, I felt we needed something we could store in the archives, something we could look back on in a few hundred years and say 'Hey that was bloody Australian'. That's why I came up with the idea to drive around for a few weeks with a tape recorder and try and record some chunks of real Australia. Stories and yarns, and bits of history from salt of the earth people, and get it down on CD. It was a pretty ambitious project but as it turned out I met some fantastic people and collected some really interesting stuff.

And if you're sitting there sucking on a café latte in some suburb somewhere, and you think the Aussie culture isn't what it used to be, if you think its heart isn't beating as strongly as it once did. Mate... you better think again.

My first stop on me archival Australiana project was a lovely gentle old lady I'd met at a function a while back, now retired in Darwin, we got together and she shared a classic recollection of some genuine cultural memorabilia. After a cup of tea and some scones the lovely old lady relaxed and opened up a bit. I half expected her to come up with one of those feel good, warm and fuzzy type yarns, something about finding an injured Kookaburra and nursing it back to health type stories. Or perhaps a love story with some dashing sergeant during the war.

But her story wasn't quite like that.

'Back in the day' she said, she ran a pub out bush and she liked things to run pretty ship shape, and there were certain standards patrons had to abide by. One of the golden rules was 'No Dogs allowed in the bar'.

Well, one day this bloke turns up and he came into the bar and he had his dog with him, and he simply refused to take it out. 'Where I go my dog goes' he reckoned.

'Well you'll have to take the dog out' the genteel publican announced, things getting a little heated.

'Well you make me' the bloke barks back.

'I can easy do that' she said.

At this stage I've got my tape recorder going and I'm on the edge of my seat wondering what happens next. The old lady's eyes searched and a cheeky smile worked its way across her face as she took a pause. A quick nibble from her scone and she slowly started up again.

'Well, he thought he was tough, and the dog thought he was tough, but they didn't know just how tough I was, so I went and got the gun and - I blew the dog out'!

The old lady let out a wild cackle, then focused again back on the story.

'And what a mess, I had to take it down to the dump and bury it', she said with some remorse. Then another wild cackle, and back to the story. 'It was hard being a publican in the bush' she reckoned,

'Sometimes people would try to take advantage of you because you were a woman, but they forgot one thing - I had a shotgun'.

I thanked her for that contribution to my project, and I had originally planned to ask her for some more memories, but I was a bit scared of what she might actually come up with, so I left it at that. I'm thinkin, that story says a lot about Australians and their ability to solve a problem.

Although the RSPCA mightn't quite support me on that one. But it was a good start to me CD.

Then I followed up a lead from a good friend's wife. Her old man had been a truckie all his life and she reckoned he had some good yarns. I tracked him down in Katherine at his quiet home not far from the river, and he agreed to give me a story for the project as well. Being a truckie driving road trains all his life he told me he went through this period where he wanted to try something totally different. Something where no one talks about gearboxes or differentials, and something that had absolutely nothing to do with truckin. So he decided to take up Skydiving.

Now, I don't know if this is a natural progression for all truckies, but anyway he loved it, Skydiving was exactly what he needed, and he jumped regularly.

On one particular occasion the local parish Priest had decided to come out for a jump as well, being a bit of an enthusiast. The priest launched himself out of the light aircraft - sailed through the air - the wind got hold of him - it blew him way off course - next minute he's heading for a landing at this pit where all the dead cattle get dumped.

He landed on a dead stinking bloated cow which blew up instantly, covering him in the worst smelling shit of all times.

This took a bit of the shine off it for the priest.

On the way back to town no one would let him ride in their cars; he had to ride in the back of a Ute. This in itself was

Australian. A very well respected member of society, a person of standing, told to just get in the back. That's Australian, because it wouldn't matter if you were Queen Elizabeth the second, or the Shah of Iran, if you smelt like shit you ride in the back. That's the traditional Australian way.

It was all good cultural stuff I was getting. When people dig my Australiana collection out of the archives in millenniums to come they're going to look back and say 'Wow, weren't they sophisticated back in those days, they were way ahead of their time.'

When a bloke sets out to collect important cultural material, there's no doubt about it, the front bar at the Pine Creek Hotel is just an oasis of culture. They come from everywhere to suck piss and immerse themselves into the art of sharing Australian cultural history. I knew I'd get some valuable stuff there, and over a few coldies one old feller gave me a really good insight into Pine Creek back in 1966.

He came to Pine Creek looking for his father, the one his mother hadn't seen for a long time. His long lost Dad was running the pub at the time and they shared a few beers, and he suggested they go to the 'Flicks' as the travelling picture show man was in town. He'd set up his screen down at the town hall.

This was a big occasion for the small Top End town of Pine Creek and everyone was there. Even a group of traditional Aboriginal men had walked in from somewhere out bush to see the movie as well. They all had their spears and boomerangs, and stood proudly at the back. The picture show cranked up, and on the big screen a 'Hop-a-long Cassidy' action western was the feature.

Remember this was in the days before T.V and everyone

was totally engrossed. Half way through the movie the hero 'Hop-a-long' was doing it tough, one of the bad guys had ambushed him and looked like he was about to shoot the star. Well, it got too much for one of the Aboriginal blokes, as the baddy drew the hammer back on his gun ready to nail Hop-a-long, the Aboriginal bloke let loose with a boomerang that whizzed and chopped through the air and tore a hole in the screen, right where the bad guy's head was. Anyway the lights came on and the show was over, but wouldn't that bloke be handy these days at the football, when the umpire makes a bad decision.

I couldn't imagine anything more Australian than taking the umpire out with a Boomerang.

Bloody hell that's Australian.

I was on a roll with my project and shortly after the Pine Creek recollections I run into a Park Ranger from Kakadu. He had an amazing story of how he went out in a small boat one night on the South Alligator River to harpoon a crocodile, in the hope of relocating it. This was the first time he'd taken part in such an operation and he was as keen as mustard. He found the croc, threw the harpoon, got tangled up in the rope fell in the water and got severely mauled, but hey, throwing yourself in the deep end is Australian.

Then I met a lady that put Icing and a few candles on a dried out Buffalo turd, and served it up as a birthday cake. Everyone was that drunk they tried to eat it.

How Australian can you get! And that story is gunna be handy to look back on in a few hundred years because no doubt there's probably going to be a few more world wars and stuff, and people might just forget what having a good time is all about.

188 The 'Minor Successes' of a Bloke Who Never Had a Real Lot of Luck

I can just see it now, surrounded by radioactive fallout from the bombs and rising seas due to global warming, they'll all be sitting around listening to me CD thinking 'shit', those old time Aussies really knew how to have a bit of fun.

When it comes to history being handed down through the generations you can't beat Aboriginal people. They're brilliant 'Orators' or storytellers and all their 40,000 plus years of history have been passed on orally. So they've had many years experience in perfecting the art of the yarn, and they can sure spin one. One Aboriginal friend of mine had a real gift for telling a story and I was over the moon to get him on the C.D.

Growing up in remote Arnhem Land he recalled the fantastic nights sitting around the fire with the old men and there were always many stories to share.

His Uncle told him of an adventure he had one day as he was walking down the one bush road, this was before the introduction of four wheel drives and motorbikes and there was just a track people and also animals would use to go through the bush he explained, then he continued. One day my uncle was walking back from hunting, he'd just speared some fish and was walking along the one bush road and he saw a Buffalo coming the other way. Buffalo can be very dangerous and unpredictable so he looked around for somewhere to hide but there was only a really small skinny tree just off the track, so he made himself skinny and got behind it. When the Buffalo walked past he jumped out in front of it and went 'HUH', and the huge Buffalo got such a shock, he fell over stone dead, he had a heart attack!

Great yarn, great history, but please don't try that one at home.

I was really enjoying collecting all this material, it made me appreciate even more what a special place Australia is and the uniqueness of the people populating it.

And of-course any excuse to travel around, but the funny thing about having a tape recorder you start listening more carefully to sounds, and you become more aware of the sounds around you. Although this project was all about collecting people's history and stories I often found myself compelled to record birds and stuff, and one time when there was a thunder storm I stood out on the flat and held the microphone skywards to tape the action. Anyone driving past would have wondered what the hell that dickhead is doing standing out there. Another time I was running through the scrub on the edge of the road at full speed with the microphone extended out in front of me trying to catch up and tape a mob of Black Cockatoos, I must have looked a little crazy because all the traffic was slowing down to see what was happening.

But this was all about capturing Australia and so I wanted as much as I could get to paint a real picture, but using sound.

It must have been sheer luck because I kept running into really interesting people, and the Archival CD was just looking better and better.

At a campground in Kakadu I bumped into good friend Jungle Jacky, she'd not long just got over being bitten by a deadly Western Brown Snake, apparently a group of tourists were swimming in this billabong and they come across the snake who must have been trying to swim across. It was a huge panic and Jungle Jacky who was nearby run over and dived in, and put herself between the snake and the group of tourists.

On one side of her were these crazed panic stricken tourists, and on the other was a crazed panic stricken deadly snake.

Anyway the snake ended up biting her twice and anyone else would have died but because she's so good looking the venom had no effect. What an amazing story of heroism in the true Australian tradition.

The tape recorder shook with emotion when it recorded that one.

Then down the track a bit I pulled into this roadhouse for a brew and I run into old mate Daniel Tapp. Daniel always had great yarns and I set the tape recorder up before I even asked him what he'd been up to, because I knew it would be something exciting. Sure enough him and an old Aboriginal bloke had been out checking a bore and the vehicle broke down, and they were stuck out there for days, no food, and they were getting pretty hungry. Daniel found a hook and a bit of fishing line and the old Aboriginal bloke cut some dried skin off the bottom of his foot for bait and so they ditched the line in at a nearby creek, and caught two Black Bream.

Daniel said it was the best feed he ever had, no salt, but she was a good feed, he reckoned.

To me that was survival Australian style, and hopefully future generations can learn a lot from that yarn.

Australia and adventure really go hand in hand, there's no doubt about it. One bloke I come across told me he'd taken the family camping out bush and in the middle of the night a huge croc goes through the side of the tent grabs his old mum in its jaws and starts swinging her around. Well everyone woke up, and instantly and in complete unison, the whole family said 'Fuck this', even the two month old newborn baby that hadn't learnt to talk yet said it. The bloke poked the croc in the eyes and it released his mum and took off.

Now that's what I call a family camping trip... Australian style.

There was no doubt about it the CD was a corker and eventually when I thought I had enough stuff on there I headed back to town. It couldn't have turned out any better and the finished Archival collection was a great Major Success.

But it was so good I thought why just donate it to the archives and libraries for prosperity straight away? I mean I'd worked really hard collecting all this stuff, why not try and make a well deserved dollar out of it first.

So I printed a fair few CD's and put them in some shops and got ready to count the money. What a great idea, should make a killing. This one is really going to be a Major Success.

But you know... the funny thing is, Australia is a great place and we've got a unique culture and everyone's fantastic and stuff, but when it comes to buying CD's... Australians are a tight fisted mob of bastards!

Once again I had to downgrade to just a Minor Success.

THE END

IF YOU'VE MADE IT ALL THE WAY through to this point in me book congratulations, and by now you probably realise 'Major Successes' are bloody hard to come by. They're as rare as rocking horse shit and they're elusive. It's o.k. to live in hope, but don't forget to be content with what you have. Success isn't everything. I've tried hundreds of different jobs, and travelled in and out of hundreds of one-horse towns searching for a Major Success, and where has it got me?

No need to really answer that one.

But Minor Successes come in all shapes and sizes and no matter how hard things get, or if times are tough, there's generally something we can take out of a situation, hold it to our hearts and say well - that little something was a Minor Success.

Shit it could have been worse. Just stay positive. Like I always said, you only live once then you're dead for a long time. If you're still alive, things aren't that bad.

Be happy for the humble everyday Minor Successes, and until we meet again somewhere - on the road - or in a pub - or the pages of a book, take a tip from me and...

Just take life one beer at a time.

GLOSSARY OF TERMS

This has been added for the benefit of anyone not familiar with the Australian language... and has no idea what we are talking about.

A COLD ONE – A can or bottle of beer

A COLDIE – A beer

A BALL-TEARER – Something out of the ordinary

A LITTLE STUNG – Reasonably intoxicated

A MATE - A good friend

A PIZZLING – To be beaten, abused

ANZAC Day – An annual celebration of Australian and New Zealand Armed Forces.

A ROLLIE – A Cigarette made by placing loose tobacco in a cigarette paper and rolling it up.

ARVO - Afternoon

A SLICE OF HEAVEN – A very enjoyable experience

A STATION – A large pastoral property

BALL BAG – A male scrotum

BARRAMUNDI – A good eating fish found in the northern waters of Australia

BATTING FOR THE OTHER TEAM - Gay

BBQ – Pronounced Barb-Bee-Que, The cooking of meat on a hotplate over a fire, generally done outdoors

BILLABONG – A body of water, a waterhole

BILLY - A container for boiling water on the open fire

BRASS – Money

BUGGER ALL – Not much, very little

BUGGERED – Very tired, exhausted

BUFF – Water buffalo

BRUMBY – Wild Horse

BURKE AND WILLS – A pair of early Australian explorers that perished tragically

CLACKER VALVE - Anus

CHAFFING AT THE BIT - Can't wait, very exited

CHEWING THE FAT - Having a conversation

CHOKED OUT - Passed out drunk or in a deep sleep, collapsed

CHOKED DOWN - Same as choked out

COPPER - A police officer

CRACK A FAT - To get an erection

DAMPER - Bush style bread cooked in the coals

DINGHY - A small boat

DOGGED IT - Given in, won't go anymore, sulking

DONE ME NUTS - Fell in love

DONE THE HAROLD HOLT - Left in a real hurry, rushed off

DUNNY - Toilet

FEELING LIKE A HALF SUCKED RICEBUBBLE - Not in good
  health, feeling poorly

FLOAT - To leave and go somewhere else

FLOATING HANDBAG - A Crocodile

FOOT FALCON - Walking as a mode of transport

FOX - To avoid the issue, to be sneaky

FRESHIE - A freshwater crocodile

GAS - Energy

GROG - Alcohol

GOANNA - A large Lizard

GOOD LIZARD COUNTRY - An area with a large crocodile
  population

GUNNED IT - Travelled very quickly, with pace

HAD ME HAND ON IT - Not being realistic

HAIR OF THE DOG - A beer drank the morning after you wake up
  with a massive hangover, a pick me up

HAPPY AS LARRY - In a very good mood

HOOT - Money

IN LIKE FLYN – Confident of having a sexual encounter

IN THE HORRORS – Not functioning very well, usually as a result of alcohol abuse

KICK HER IN THE GUTS – Start the motor

KIMBERLEY – A large area of rugged sparsely populated country situated in Australia's remote northwest

KNEE TREMBLER – Trying to have sex whilst standing up

LEAD IN THE PENCIL – Feeling energetic

LETTING THE FERRET OUT FOR A RUN – Exposing the male sex organ

MOB – A group, or a collection

MOZZIE – Mosquito

MUSTER CATTLE – To gather cattle together and bring to a central place

NO RIVER MURRAY'S – Not a problem, easy

OLD FELLA – A penis

PLAN B – The next thing you try after the original idea has failed

PHAR LAP – Legendary Australian race horse

PISS - Alcohol

PISS UP – A Party

PISS TANK – Someone who consumes a lot of alcohol

PISSED - Drunk

PISS OFF – To leave, also can be used as a warning

PIECE OFF PISS – Something that is very easy to achieve, no problems

PIG ROOT – The bucking motion of a horse

PLUMS – A Males Testicles

POMMY – Someone from England

PULLED OUT – finished up, departed

PUT THE NOSEBAG ON – To eat a meal

PUT THE CUE IN THE RACK – To die

PRETTY TOEY - Restless

ROOTED – Extremely tired, can't go on

ROUGH AS GUTS – Not very well presented

SLAB – A carton of beer

STYLE UP – To move to a higher standard

STONY BROKE – No money at all,

STUBBY – A glass bottle containing beer

SUCK PISS – To drink alcohol

SERVO – A Place to obtain fuel

SLIM DUSTY – A famous Australian country music singer

SMOKO – A short break, a rest

SPEW – To vomit

SPARROW FART – Very early in the morning

SUGAR HER UP – The process of impressing a female

SUGERED – A female that has been suitably impressed

SWAG – A Bedroll, something to sleep on

THE 'DO' – A party or a function of some sort

THE DON – A great Australian cricket player of renown

THE GOOD OIL – Valuable information

THE FULL BOTTLE – Knowledgeable, an expert

THE SHITHOUSE - Toilet

TIGHTEN THE BELT – Stop spending so much money,
  live more economically

TINNY – A small aluminium boat

TO RATTLE SOMEONES CAGE – To upset someone, to annoy
  someone

TRUE BLUE – Genuine, 100% Australian

TWITCHY – To get nervous

UNDER THE PUMP – Feeling pressured, under stress

WILLY WILLY – A strong spiralling gust of wind

YARN – a story or a description of an event

ALSO BY PHIL O'BRIEN

'101 ADVENTURES THAT GOT ME ABSOLUTELY NOWHERE' Paperback

The Australian landscape whipped past the windows of the Greyhound bus. 'I'm going places.' I thought. 'I'm gunna take the bush by storm. I'm gunna ride everything. break in everything. dehorn everything and make love to ANYTHING'. Join Phil O'Brien on his hilarious travels as he ventures from Kimberley to Kakadu looking for adventure. and love. in all the wrong places.

'101 ADVENTURES... SONGS AND STORIES'
Audio 2x C.D

An audio version of 101 Adventures... spoken by Phil O'Brien and also containing a bunch of original songs performed in between yarns.

'YARNS FROM THE WILD TOP END'
Audio C.D

The Top End is no ordinary place and neither are the people who live there. In this collection of yarns. Phil O'Brien and his tape recorder captures the passion. danger and exotica of Top End Territory and the eclectic group of people who live there. There are yarns about croc attacks. imaginary friends. women who run pubs out the back of nowhere and daring rescues through shark infested waters. It is an extraordinary place where extraordinary things happen.

Available at any good book shop
Or - Mail Order Enquiries to Phil O'Brien
Box 257 Katherine 0850
Northern Territory. Australia
Email campfiresinger@hotmail.com